With masterful sto  Rosseland's *Angels Among Us* invites you into the lives of real people who have been touched by God's celestial messengers. Whether you're an angel believer or you're skeptically hopeful they exist, these stories of healing, comfort, and protection will convince you there's more to this life than what you can see. Prepare for your heart to be stirred, your eyes to warm with tears, and your soul to thrum with greater awareness of God's mysterious ways.

> Sarah Forgrave, author of *Prayers for Hope and Healing:*
> *Seeking God's Strength as You Face Health Challenges*

Join Wanda Rosseland as she takes you on a celestial tour of heavenly messengers. These angels are the real deal. Like Wanda.

> Rick Hamlin, executive editor of *Guideposts* magazine
> and author of *Pray for Me*.

Angels
AMONG US

Angels
AMONG US

EXTRAORDINARY ENCOUNTERS
WITH HEAVENLY
BEINGS

Wanda Rosseland

WORTHY®
Inspired

Library of Congress Control Number: 2017943807

ISBN: 978-1-68397-051-4

With thanks to God

who sees fit

to have faith in us still

after all these years.

CONTENTS

INTRODUCTION

In the latter days of 1992, I had no intention of writing a book. Most especially one on angels, those ethereal and somewhat mysterious messengers of God who strangely possess the ability to melt through doors and hearts alike.

I was just an ordinary farmwife, waking each morning to fix our breakfast, feed the cows, and enjoy the peaceful winter days on our quiet Montana farm. It was Christmas, and we were going to see our daughter—not receive instructions from God. At least, that's what I thought.

A short three days before, Jeannie had called home, trying hard not to cry. Seven and a half months pregnant with her first child, she told us the doctors had decided the baby must be born. Two weeks earlier, while driving on an icy road, a vehicle spun out in front of her as it tried to enter the road from a side street. Jeannie frantically pumped the brakes to stop, but it was no use. The ice was as slick as a skating rink under her tires, and she slid straight toward the van, slamming into it broadside. At first, the collision did not appear to injure her unborn child, but further tests showed that he had stopped growing.

"They're afraid to leave him any longer, Mom," she worried, "in case he has brain damage."

An icicle stabbed my heart. Two babies we'd buried, and the pain of their loss never lessened. What would happen now to this, our grandson? Would he live, only to be unable to read or write his name, or would we gather again around fresh spaded earth?

Four hundred miles away, with one hundred cows to care for in the dead of winter, and up-thrusts of the Rocky Mountains between us, my husband, Milton, and I could not leave instantly to be with her. So I did what I've learned to do when I'm helpless, I fell in my chair and began praying.

Dear God, please help Jeannie. Protect her baby, stand beside him while he is being born, and let his mind be uninjured. Please Lord, let him walk and talk and run and laugh like every other normal child. Hold him in your hands and place your angels around them both, to keep them safe. In Jesus' name I pray. Amen

The next morning, Scott came into this world healthy and well. Small, jaundiced, but with ten fingers and itsy toes and eyes that seemed to peer out of a thousand-year-old soul. Because Jeannie and her husband had planned on coming home for Christmas, we had all their presents, along with the turkey, tree, and my family invited down for dinner. But now, with Scott so new and in such fragile health, it was impossible for them to take him out in the cold and jeopardize his life by trying to drive across the state of Montana in the middle of the winter. Perhaps they could not be with us, but with luck, we could go to them. Milton and I looked at the display around the living room and said, "We're going."

Putting out a double feed of chopped hay and barley for the cows, we unrolled bales of straw for them to sleep on, called my mother to cancel festivities and headed west, taking the shortest route through the hills from Circle to Bozeman. We got there in time to have Christmas dinner with them all and gently hold our little grandson. He was the best present under the tree.

Early the next day we started for home and decided to swing through Billings in order to stop at my twin sister Rita's house and say "Merry Christmas," knowing we would not get back to see her before spring. She brought us into her cozy apartment, warmed us with tea and cookies, and after congratulating us on our first grandchild, she began to tell me about a man I did not know, Gary Heidner, the brother of one of our high school classmates in Wolf Point.

Gary had been diagnosed with cancer and was operated on to remove a tumor from his brain earlier in the month. When Rita heard about it, she went up to see him in the hospital.

On this 26th day of December, relieved that our daughter and her baby were both doing fine, and concerned only with driving the last 250 miles home without a blizzard overtaking us, I had just taken another sip of warm tea when through the haze, I heard Rita saying, ". . . before his operation, his wife saw angels. There was a row of angels surrounding the bed where she lay."

Every cell in my being snapped to attention. I sat on the couch stupefied, knowing instantly I was to write this story, that it had been given to me expressly by God to do so . . . and I was inadequate.

There was no way I could write a book. Little things, yes, like the articles I did for magazines, short pieces, a thousand words, those I could handle. But this? On angels?

Quaking inside, I carefully lowered the china cup onto its saucer, leaned forward to set them on the coffee table before my trembling hands dropped them, and placed the half-eaten cookie on the napkin beside them.

"Rita," I forced out. "Can you tell me more?"

"I don't know any more," she said, getting up and stepping into the kitchen. "But I've got Rhonda's phone number right here. You can ask her."

Like a wooden robot, I took the slip of paper and pushed it down deep in the pocket of my purse, willing myself to stop shaking, to keep her from seeing the irrational fear that swelled up inside me. What did I know of angels? Who was I to tell another's story? Who was I to tell God's?

Of course I knew they existed, had seen paintings of their great majestic beauty, the wings which carried them from heaven and back, how could God put wings on a body like us and make it look right, anyway? That was a miracle in itself.

I'd read their accounts in the Bible, most notably of the ones who announced the birth of the Christ Child, Jesus our Saviour. And every now and then a magazine would publish a story, usually at Christmas time, which told of someone seeing angels or being inexplicably saved by them. But me? Qualified to write about them? I was far from it. The articles I wrote covered farming and agriculture, subjects I was familiar with since we grew wheat and raised cattle on our place in Montana. But never once had I considered writing about angels.

I left Rita's house shaken, certain I could not carry out this great charge. That I was not worthy to be entrusted with it. All that winter, I vacillated between calling Rhonda or putting it off. How would you like to have a stranger on the phone, asking about your husband while he was fighting for his life? I felt like an intruder, hard and selfish, without care or consideration for her pain and suffering. Still, the certainty that God had assigned me to do this persisted.

The days lengthened as spring came. We went through calving, seeding, haying, all the summer months of the next year while I invented reasons to walk past the phone. Finally I made myself do it. Rhonda herself said, "Hello."

She was gracious, forthright and matter of fact about telling me what had happened. She treated me like a friend, rather than someone she had never met, and I was humbled by both her faith and generosity. Without pause or questioning, she told me of the coming of the angels and how they had given both her and Gary peace and comfort as he fought his illness.

After we finished talking, I sat at the oak table in the office, filling in the notes I had taken by hand. *I wonder what God has to say about this?* I thought. How could I know? God rarely talks open mouthed to me, but sometimes He instructs through His Word, the Holy Bible, and I have learned to search for His direction there. This I would do now.

Going to the other room, I picked up the tattered white Bible our widowed farm neighbor had given me for our high school graduation, years before. Laying it on the table, I closed my eyes, asked God what He wanted me to do and opened it to a random page. Looking down, my eyes fell upon this verse:

> *Write thee all the words that I have*
> *spoken unto thee in a book.*
> Jeremiah 30:2

Sounded like an order to me.

RHONDA

Through the ages, angels have usually been identified by their dazzling white robes and magnificent wings, but in actuality they can come to us in various forms. Some take the build of our human bodies, looking exactly like a normal person, who helps, heals, or stands as a protector for another, but then suddenly, inexplicably, disappears. Others are perceived as lights, beautiful colors of the rainbow darting about a room like the light refracted from crystals hanging in a window pane. Sometimes they can be heard with the ear, new voices joining the choir while hymns are being sung in church, when there is no one to be seen, while others even less distinct are recognized by their smell, the sweet soft perfume of roses, or the fragrance of delicate orange blossoms.

To Rhonda, they appeared as a softly flowing arch, indistinct, without form, yet visible and discernible and very, very real.

"They were angels," she says, and in her voice was the certainty of knowing.

Rhonda and her husband, Gary, had been fighting his cancer for some time. Starting first as melanoma, the dangerous skin cancer which can quickly spread to other parts of the body, they had treated him as carefully as possible, hoping to stop any further growth. But without their knowledge, the cancer turned inward, attacking Gary's organs and eventually traveling to his brain. Intense headaches, accompanied with severe nausea and pain, took them to the hospital again, where tests revealed a malignant tumor.

Dedicated schoolteachers in Billings, with a young family to care for, neither one was prepared for the brusque and thoughtless manner of the physician who told them of this new threat to his life. A hard note of anger slipped into Rhonda's voice as she remembered the day and the way he had treated them.

"He wasn't very good about it," she stated. "He just said straight out, 'You have a golf-ball-sized brain tumor.'

"Gary said, 'What!'

"'You've got a tumor,' the doctor repeated. 'You'll have to see the neurosurgeon tomorrow.'"

Gary and Rhonda sat stunned, unable to absorb this devastating news. For six weeks, the headaches had bothered him but never once had they associated them with cancer. And certainly not a brain tumor.

Struggling to hold themselves together, they went home, asked her parents to take their children for the night so they could be alone, and then collapsed in disbelief, overwhelmed at the severe advances the cancer had taken. Unsuspecting, they'd been blindsided. Deep despair and helplessness filled them, leaving them numb and barely able to function.

"We talked . . . cried," said Rhonda, remembering that long night. "Gary was fairly calm," she added, "though now I realize he was still in shock. I made tea for us and we drank it and asked each other, 'What are we going to do?' We decided we would just do what we had to—go in the next day and do whatever the doctors said.

"Gary was put on medicine to reduce the swelling of the tumor before he saw the doctors," said Rhonda. "He laid down but couldn't rest very well because of the severity of the tumor. About two a.m. he got up, went down to the living room and started going over our insurance policy, trying to see what it would cover. He was really just tidying things up."

Rhonda sat by him, ready to help in any way she could. Finally around three o'clock, she decided to go to bed.

"I went into the bedroom, closed my eyes and tried *really* hard to go to sleep. But I couldn't. I kept thinking, 'I've got to get some rest because I have to support Gary.'"

Keyed up with worries and fear over the impending operation, her eyes refused to obey her mind as she lay, sleepless, staring up at the ceiling.

"The room was dark," she recalled. "A little lighter with

the light on in the living room than it would have been otherwise. I was looking straight up over our bed when I saw a white, swirling substance, kind of like clouds.

"Immediately I thought, *I'm seeing angels!* But I couldn't believe it was so. I closed my eyes and wiped them with my hand, but when I looked again, they were still there.

"A great calmness came over me—and I am not a calm person. I remember thinking, *We're going to be all right. We're going to get through this.* I was so incredibly peaceful. I didn't hear voices or anything, but I felt a Presence. And I *knew* I was not asleep. And I was not dreaming because I wiped my eyes and everything.

"The angels were like an arch up over our bed, a swirling light, much lighter colored than anything else around me. There were no faces, or any distinction of any kind, but it was what you would think of as a spirit being. It wasn't one angel, I think it was several.

"After they disappeared, I was wide awake, and so alert I got up and went down to Gary. But it wasn't until we were in the waiting room at the doctor's office the next day that I told him what had happened. 'You're not going to believe me,'" I said, 'but I saw angels last night.'

"He looked at me funny and said, 'You know that song, *Angels Watching Over Me*, it's been going through my head all day. I can't get it out of my mind.'

"He was in surgery the following day, December 17th,

1992, to remove the tumor and afterwards I brought the tape up with the song on it, and he told me, 'Those songs make me feel so much better.'"

While Gary was in surgery, Rhonda told several friends, who had come to the hospital to keep her company, that angels had visited her the night before. One was the pastor of their church.

"You know, Pastor," Rhonda said. "I am not a very charismatic Christian, but I swear I saw angels last night.

"Some friends looked at me, stunned. One said, 'I was praying for you and Gary and I had my hands folded. They became so hot I had to separate them, I could not keep them together.'

"Another said, 'Prayers are hard for me to say, I can't get the words right. But I was praying for you and Gary and the thoughts and phrases that came to mind were like something you would hear a pastor say.'"

Throughout his recovery, angels of different sorts continued to comfort Gary. The year before, a little girl who found out she needed a bone marrow transplant had been a student in Gary's fourth-grade class. She was really smart and loved working with the computers in Gary's classes. After she got cancer, she told her mother she wished she could have a computer. As soon as Gary heard about it, he contacted some computer companies and found out they had a "Make a Wish" program. One of the companies called

Gary and said, "We got your letter about Samantha and were so touched we are sending her a computer." They gave her a laptop, so she could use it in the hospital.

"He always wished he could do more for Samantha," said Rhonda. "I remember him saying, 'Now I know what the Spirit of Giving is all about.' We felt so bad that the treatments did not heal Samantha and she passed away in June of 1992."

When Samantha's mother went up to the hospital to see Gary after his brain surgery, she left him a card saying, *Remember, your little guardian angel in Heaven, Samantha, is looking after you.* And she gave him a raffia angel which Rhonda hung so Gary could see it from his bed.

Another person who came to see Gary was one of his sister's high-school classmates from Wolf Point. Rita walked in and Gary thought, *I don't remember this person, she was a friend of my sister's. What am I going to talk about with her?* But he told Rhonda they had the best conversation. She said, "I'm writing a book and guess what the title is? *Angel Talk.*"

It was like the third time angels had come up since he'd been in the hospital.

Rhonda and Gary could hardly believe all of these angels were coincidence. They had to have come from God to help them.

"We said this has to be Divine Presence," recalled Rhonda. "The feeling of calmness that we both had the whole time Gary was sick could not have been found any other way."

Gary survived his brain surgery but the cancer was unrelenting, forcing him to undergo two more operations, one in Billings and the other in Rochester, Minnesota. A short seven months after his initial diagnosis, he was once again back in the hospital in Billings, where Rhonda asked him if there was anything she could bring him.

"Yes," he replied. "I want my angel." The little raffia angel Samantha's mother had given him after his first operation. Rhonda brought it up for him and set it so he could see it easily from his bed.

That night she went home, alone one more time and unable to sleep, knowing in her heart Gary's fight with cancer would not be won.

"I was reading the Bible and praying for strength and guidance to help us through these next few days. I was really wanting things to be calmer," she said, "when suddenly I saw the swirling arch over my bed and I knew it was the angels.

"I thought, *I should call Gary and tell him the angels are back.* But it was four in the morning, and I didn't want to disturb him. When I went in the next day, he said, 'You should have called. I was thinking of you at the same time.'

"I felt like they were saying, '*We're still with you.*'" said Rhonda. "They were so vivid, and the tranquility that came over me was like I have never felt. Way, way up at the top of the ceiling, there was nothing. But a foot below, and down to about three feet above the bed, it was filled with angels. There was no noise. No vibration. But the light. It was a sort of pearly gray over-light, with white in it. Not brilliant like sunlight or streams through a cloud. Just a light that couldn't be there. Because it was impossible."

In that room. In the middle of the night. In the depths of darkness. Where no light shone except for that brought on the wings of angels. With a peace that never left her, even after Gary's death.

GAIL

How do I know when God is going to give me angel stories?

They come from the the most unexpected places and are always a jolt to my system. Zap! I snatch paper and pen, scribble words I cannot read later and pray God to let me remember.

Some lucky times I've got a recorder. "Wait! Wait!" I cry, punching buttons, turning knobs. "Let me get this thing going." They sit with the patience of a mother placidly watching her child, while I quail beneath God's commandings. *Get on with it!* I try, knowing I will never be qualified, and frantically wonder why He has chosen *me* to do this.

Such was the case with Gail.

In the cool evening of November 29, 1997, Mother drove down from the farm to go with me to Sannie and Johnny's 50th wedding anniversary. Daddy's sister, Sannie had been Mother's best friend when Mom worked at QB&R in Glendive just out of business college. A bubbling extrovert, she raised three boys and a girl on their farm, along with a flourishing garden and henhouse full of cockerels. In the summer, we girl cousins took turns going over to help.

This night Mom and I snuck down the hallway of the church, hushed before the program already begun, and stood in the doorway of the room, letting our eyes adjust to the light. My brother Clinton, seated at the big round table in the back with all the cousins from Billings—Tommy, Duane, Jerry, and Bob, waved us over.

I saw their faces, the smiles so big and welcome, and steered Mother toward the chairs, just two, side by side, which seem to be waiting for us. The cousins open their arms with hugs that will never change.

Sannie is talking, telling stories on all the children, who take over the mike after each completion to add their correction. "No Mother, I did *not* leave the plug out of the tractor. The o-ring was nicked and allowed the oil to drip out."

Sheepishly, "Dad did spank us—once. We had the choice of Mom's metal ruler or Dad, and took him. Never again." To much laughter.

As at every holiday in the past, we call for songs, with Sannie and Johnny playing the piano and violin as they did at the Christmases, Thanksgivings, Fourth's of July when five or six or seven of Grandma's children and all the cousins gathered.

The buzz of friends and relatives stretches across the room as a line starts at the buffet and little blonde-haired grandchildren begin to dance around the tables to the music.

How many times have I heard those songs? Watched the two heads turned toward each other, listening to the beat, synchronizing the rhythm, while fingers unerringly touch each chord, every note on ivory and strings.

Suddenly I am not there, in a crowded church room lit by greenish fluorescent lights. Instead, it is 1955 and I am in Grandpa's house, the one from Montgomery Ward that was built on the homestead near Bloomfield, twirling on the maple floor to a schottische my heart will always remember. I would know it in New York, Chicago.

"Mother! What is the name of that song?" I cry, turning to her, expecting an instant answer because she has heard it, played it too, how many times? And her eyes go back, searching along lost trails in a desperate effort to remember.

"I don't know." The failure sounds in her voice, the shake of her head as her eyes meet mine in a kind of denial that tears through my soul.

Quick tears scratch my throat, clamoring to be let loose, and I swivel in one smooth move away from her view so that she cannot see me crying for her before she is gone.

My cousin Shauna, adopted and raised by her grand-parents after the death of her mother, slips into an empty chair beside us and wraps Mother in her arms. Her gentle sweetness reaches over to soothe me, and I am able to bring up a smile. Behind our greeting I catch the edge of her older sister Gail, weaving towards us through the ribbons and balloons.

Once full of promise, the freshness that was Gail has been dulled and lost through years of hopelessness and unrelenting disappointments. The thickening of middle age shortens her natural stockiness and adds to the poverty draping her like a faded curtain. Worn-out shoes, baggy pants, a hideous blouse that apparently doubles for party wear. Even so, she's grinning, obviously very happy to see us.

I remember the Gail I loved as a child. Rollicking, full of laughter, always thrilled to see us, and I determine to meet her joy for joy and hug her over the scraggly hair. Peering at me through outdated glasses, she immediately asks, "Wanda, can you give me a ride home?"

I'm aghast. Is this the only reason she's come over? Something clicks and I realize the courage it has taken for her to just show up, having become what many would call a failure amongst her family of peers, most of whom have done well and are successful. She is not. What *is* her home? Can she even drive? I doubt she has a license and know she doesn't own a car.

"Sure, Gail," I say, "Let's go." Telling Mom I will be back shortly, we walk to my car, me shivering in my heavy winter coat, her not even noticing she doesn't have one on. In the light of the inside bulb, she thrusts a folded paper at me. "He just died," she says. "His funeral was yesterday."

I look down to a memorial brochure, the florid face of a once handsome man smiling at me. "We were going to be married," she added. "He loved me."

Dear God. What can I say to this woman who has just lost the last hope and security of her life?

"I'm so sorry, Gail," sounds shallow even to me, but she passes over it as if I have not spoken and begins to talk about what they had planned together, how they were so happy and looking forward to being married.

I drive the streets to her intermittent directions and pull up at what would be a darling gingerbread house if only it was kept up. Two windows flank the door, square in the center, with piles of old bicycles and trash littering the porch.

My fingers itch for a paintbrush as we push inside the room, to a home crying for care. Bare sheetrock, smoke and water stained, is nailed to the walls. Sporadic pictures, making a brave effort to produce cheer, hang crooked on its surface.

In the kitchen, days of dishes holding the remains of past breakfasts and suppers sit dried and hardened, stacked askew on every counter and overflowing to the metal table, while pots with unrecognizable contents fall off the burners on the stove.

A path, somehow shoveled through the living room, ends at a chair, remarkably empty, which Gail sinks into with the familiarity of old friends. Although there is only one ancient couch, totally covered with boxes, pictures, clothing, books and a miniature organ, the kind of which I last saw in 1964, Gail waves her hand and tells me to sit down.

Oh, Gail! My heart cracks as I continue to stand in the midst of the disorder, wondering how on earth I could do so. *How did this happen to you? What could we have done to save you?*

Gail picks up a skein of yarn, tosses it aside and announces without preamble, "I had a vision once. I saw angels."

My thoughts sprang back to her. *Gail? Angels?* Her faded blue eyes hold mine with complete openness and honesty. An arm drops to her lap. "I was about fifteen or sixteen years old and I'd gone out to milk the cows. It was at Aunt Sannie's, at night."

I can see Gail, the farmer's daughter, always trying, and being given more work for her reward. Asked to hoe, can, plunk chickens in steaming water, pull feathers, wash dishes, churn butter, and of course, milk the cows. I envision the moon, shining on the roof of the barn, her stopping to look up at the stars as you do every night when you go out to milk because they are too beautiful, too wondrous to ignore.

"I was carrying the milk buckets," she continued, "when the heavens just opened up." She glanced at her hands, like she was feeling again the cool smooth handles of the galvanized tin and repeated quietly, as if she still couldn't quite believe it. "The heavens just opened up." in a breath of a whisper.

She paused, caught in the magnificence of this remembering, then started again. "The stairway went all the way to heaven. It was big, by the barn." And like a flash, I see Gail awestruck, buckets tumbled at her sides, staring up at a white marble staircase curving to Heaven, stretching smaller and smaller until it disappeared in the sky, dwarfing herself, and all of Earth, beside it.

"They were people," she resumed decisively, as if certain I would question her and somehow convince us both that what she had seen was actually not so.

"There was a big light. The people were going down and up, and I stood and watched them."

At once, I noticed she used the word "down" before "up." Why did she place more importance on the ones going down than those ascending? It was a small distinction, but one that caused me to think for the first time that perhaps she had really seen this.

Then she stopped, looked directly at me as if it was very important I understand this, and said, "The people going down, they were angels without wings."

I was flabbergasted, my brain jumbled with shock. *Angels? Without wings?* How could she know, unless God imprinted it on her heart? She must have seen instinctively, with that second sight, the inner eye no man can detect but which is real and exists nonetheless.

And where were the angels going? To assist us human

beings? To those believers admonished by Paul in Hebrews 13:2, *Be not forgetful to entertain strangers: for thereby some have entertained angels unawares*? A picture of purposeful silent figures holding their bodies regally erect fills my mind. They drift up and down the staircase, ignoring all others in passing, intent only on fulfilling their own mission.

I jerk back to Gail, as the intensity of her eyes melts away and her whole body relaxes against the chair. "Gail!" I insist. "Tell me more!" But she looks past me to another time, asserting with quiet authority an incident which shocks me nearly as much. "I saw Mac after he died."

Mac! I haven't heard his name in fifteen years. Our uncle, Daddy's brother, the oldest of the family, Mac was handsome, hardworking but an incurable alcoholic who left us too early. Gail acts like she knows I need this validation, to differentiate between angels and real people.

"The day he died, I looked up and saw him coming toward me. I said, 'Mac!' and held out my hand. He passed through it like I wasn't even there. He was transparent," she explained, lifting her eyes to see if I understood, "I could see right through him."

Shaking her head, she said with sorrow, "I knew he was dead before anyone else did." She was eight years old at the time.

Though I try, it is useless to ask for more. She is done, lapsed back in her chair, the old apathy taking over. I recognize defeat and turn to leave.

Was it Sannie and Johnny's anniversary that brought it all to mind? Was it the unexpected death of her loved one? Or did God just say, "It is time. Tell her the story of the angels"?

Whatever the reason, she has done what she is supposed to do, now I must do mine. I drive out of the yard, stop under the first streetlight, dig out my pen and start writing.

GRANDMA MASSAR

G randma Massar lived across the street from us in an old Victorian house with gabled ends and an evergreen roof. I both loved and hated to go see her, she scared me so much with her severe unbending ways, but nowhere in Circle, Montana was there such a wonderful bed of soft velvet pansies.

For them I would cautiously lift the gate latch, squat down on the concrete walk and, hands carefully clasped in my lap to keep from reaching out, feast on those happy purple petals, while Grandma stood tall and stern behind me watching. *Don't touch!* In all the years we lived in Circle, I never picked one once. Grandma did not belong to our family, but she helped Mother however she could with us eight children and every year she made sure we attended the annual week of Sunday School at church.

Sometimes I went over with Mother to visit in the hot afternoons, but mostly my older sisters, Betsy and Patsy, did. Grandma served tea in her enameled kitchen, loose leaves steeped in a pot of just-boiled water, which left them mysteriously floating in bone china cups, and cookies set out on a flower patterned plate. We were expected to sit up straight, be quiet and not drop a crumb. We didn't. We were company, in her house.

Her children were all older than us. Only the youngest, a dark-haired beauty we reverently adored, laughed and waved from the upstairs window. One son auctioneered, rolling words off his tongue in a musical sing-song that left us mesmerized.

Twenty years later, when he returned to sell the house at public auction after both Grandma and Grandpa Massar had died, I walked one last time through the darkened rooms, the south-facing living room whose shades were perpetually pulled to keep the sun off the rug, admired again the dining room chandelier, a beautiful work of hand blown glass and polished brass, hanging high with its original bulbs which amazingly still worked. The stairway I had never climbed on the far wall went up to the second floor. There, bedrooms flowed around a center hall like the points on a compass—east, south, west, each one bare now with echoing wooden floors and ghosts of laughter.

The dishes, the chairs, the spirit of Grandma hung in the air. I could see her plain cotton dress with the long skirt nearly touching the tops of her shoes as she stepped up the outside stairs, the gunmetal braid tightly wound in a bun at the back of her neck, the half-smile, playing at her mouth as if asking for a release, and rarely getting it, the sparse words, metered out with care like a shopkeeper giving change.

And as I became a teenager, I heard the murmurings of a child lost. One of Grandma's daughters, thought to have contracted tuberculosis from the cows Grandpa Massar kept in his dairy. A girl I never knew. Tuberculosis then was a feared disease because it could be transferred to humans through the cow's milk. My own grandfather, mother's dad, left his home in Kentucky as a young man to travel to the piney woods of Montana because of it, and thankfully was healed. In the early 1900s however, children especially were susceptible to tuberculosis and almost always died.

I had neither thought nor heard of Grandma Massar in years when my sister, Mary Ann, called in June of 2000 from her home in Grass Range, Montana to propose a visit to our sister, Patsy and her husband, Bud, near Yakima, Washington, where they had just built a new home.

"We can take Mother," Mary Ann suggested, "and stop and see Rex in Spokane on the way through." Our youngest brother, Rex had shortly before moved to Spokane, Washington so it was a perfect chance to see him again. By the time we finished planning, the trip had evolved into a mini family reunion, which included visiting our daughter, Kristi, where she worked in Helena, Montana, and meeting our big sister, Betsy, who was flying in to Spokane from Elko, Nevada to join us for the final leg into Yakima.

Mary Ann and I gathered up Mother and we hummed across Montana, prompting Mother to tell us stories about growing up on the ranch outside of Jordan. We stopped at

Helena to have a delightful lunch with Kristi, and swung across the river at Spokane into Rex's, where we feasted on fresh huckleberry pie he pulled out of the oven. After getting Betsy off the airplane, we swapped drivers the next day to finish the run into Bud and Patsy's at Yakima.

The stately trees of Bud's orchard, swelling with apples, and cherries just beginning to ripen, encircled their beautiful new home. We examined every nook and then sank onto Patsy's super-soft couch, continuing tales of childhood and beyond as darkness settled through the windows and my eyes began to drift shut.

Around midnight, Patsy perked up. "Do you guys remember Grandma Massar?" she asked. "She had a little girl that saw angels."

I shot up out of the tapestry and grabbed onto the arm of the couch. "What are you talking about, Patsy? Angels?"

Patsy glanced over at me with a puzzled look. "Didn't you know? The girl that died?"

The old whispers came back, slowly pulling away like fog on the river. I groped through them, the odd conversation, something about death and loss and Grandma Massar. But angels?

"Did any of you know?" I turned to Betsy, Mary Ann. They shook their heads in silence, as bewildered as I.

"Then tell us," I said, and Patsy started out.

"Grandma Massar, our neighbor who lived right next

door, sold us hay for our Brown Swiss cow, Twink, and took us to Sunday School.

"Her house had that strange smell of old houses, metal, from her cupboards I think, and appliances."

"It was musty," said Betsy.

"Yes," interjected Mary Ann. "It needed air."

"One day I went over and she seemed to want to chat," continued Patsy. "We were in her dark living room, and she was talking to me about her daughter, her little girl who had died, at the age of eight or so, from TB.

"Grandma Massar took me upstairs, to the bedroom, which was this little girl's, and she said, 'She died in this room. She died in this bed.'

"I was probably eight or nine at the time, real close to the same age, in fact I wonder now if that isn't why she told me about it.

"Then Grandma Massar said, 'When she was very sick, and we knew she was probably going to die, but we kept praying that she wouldn't, she was in a lot of pain and wasn't doing well. All of a sudden, she got this smile on her face and said, 'Look, Mom! The angels are here!'

"'I turned around and said . . .'" Here, Patsy paused.

"What was her name?" she murmured. "Do you remember, Mom?" But Mother could not recall.

"Well," Patsy continued, "Grandma said her name, and asked her, 'What do you mean?'

"The little girl replied, 'Up there in the corner. Can't you see them? There they are. They've come for me.'

"'Then I knew she was going to die,' said Grandma. 'And she did. She died.'"

We sat in silence, each one of us a mother, wondering what we would have done if it had been our child, trying to imagine the great loss Grandma Massar must have felt, not just then, but all through the rest of the years of living without her daughter.

But the grief somewhat lessened by the wonderment of her daughter seeing angels, allowing her to approach death not with fear and dread, but with joy and gladness, with the assurance of being carried back to heaven in their arms.

When I returned home to Circle, I took another little trip, across the concrete slab on the Redwater River, around the corner to the cemetery. There a small, grassy plot testified to the death of Grandma's daughter.

An old forged fence with iron swags separated a group of graves into a close square where an ancient lilac bush, grown wide from years, graced one lonely corner. I like to think Grandma planted it there so flowers would bloom every spring for her child.

Of the headstones, one stood worn, a little lamb resting quietly, his legs folded under, head up, watching, just like hundreds of live ones I've seen dotting the green pastures of Montana in the spring. But this one remains still, carved at the top of the slate-gray marker, a protector for the little girl who would never again run in Montana.

Beneath a flowering lily etched on the stone, I found her first name only.

ALICE

in bold letters, followed by:

1918–1928

OUR DARLING

The words chiseled by hand and slowly erased through nearly a century of wind and rain, so worn I had to follow them with my hand to be sure of the writing.

How was it this little girl lived and died so quickly, a brief flame of light topping a candle, snuffed out before the heat could melt the wax? I think of all the years Grandpa Massar gave as deacon to the Lutheran Church and the many headstones he must have ordered for bereaved families. Possibly the first ever was for his own child, Alice. What heartache we have to bear.

Going home, I called Marjorie, Grandma's daughter-in-law, to see if she had ever heard about an angel coming for Alice.

"Did this really happen?" I asked.

"Oh, yes," said Marjorie. "Grandma told me many times of the angel. It was a great comfort to her. Alice saw it standing in the corner of her room, it had the bright lights associated with angels. She only saw it the one time, just before she died."

"You know," she added, "Grandma held things very lightly on this earth. Her children were very important to her, but things—they are passing. She had told her daughter about Jesus of course, and she knew her little girl was with the Lord. I think the angel helped her accept her death."

"Was it tuberculosis that Alice had?"

"They were never sure," she said sadly. "Alice had a cough for so long, and the flushed look. The doctors did everything they could, but it was no good. She lingered a long time and finally passed away."

I thanked Marjorie and hung up the phone, sitting quietly in my room, thinking of that sick little girl and the desperate mother, each given a light of hope, of expectation, in those last hopeless moments, by the bright shining angels, standing with love, waiting to take Alice home.

MOTHER

My mother ruled her household with a firm "No" and an insistence on obedience. Perhaps raising her children at a home on the creek bank required it. If she hollered, "Get away from that creek right now!" she had to know we'd obey, and we knew we'd better. We did.

Mother cooked wonderful meals for us morning, noon and night, and during the summer canned hundreds of jars of fresh food. Golden peaches and red ripe cherries, along with green beans, tomatoes, and sharp cucumber pickles, vegetables fresh picked from the garden to fill the pantry shelves for the cold winter months. Her pedal Singer sewing machine sang through the days as she kept us in pants and dresses, somehow knowing just when to turn and snatch pins out of inquisitive fingers before they disappeared into open mouths.

When we lay sick in bed, vomiting and burning with fever, she spooned chicken soup into our sore throats and laid a cool, wet cloth on our forehead that felt like heaven. By her acts, we knew that she loved us.

A child of the Depression, Mother was bent and shaped in its ceaseless want, so that when she became an adult and married, only necessities filled her life. What was important mattered. Friends, family, food, clothing. With dishes to wash, diapers on the line, she rose early each day to get started on her work and ended it at midnight mopping the floor. Seeing to the well-being of her family left no time for introspection or escape to a higher plane. Angels were not a consideration.

So it was with some shock I listened to my sister, Betsy tell about Mother seeing—something—in the summer of '95.

"She called it a Spirit," Betsy explained. "She didn't know what it was, but it was real."

Only rarely did Betsy get to come back to Montana from her home in Elko, Nevada, and today she would be leaving. Yet, in our short visit the day before, she had not mentioned Mother seeing such a strange thing as a "Spirit." I eyed her across the table and set down the teapot.

"How did you learn about this?" I asked.

"Rita told me. She said Mom was very concerned, not really fearful, but uneasy about it."

Yes, I was sure Mother *would* be uneasy about something unexplainable, her gifted with an analytical mind more suited to the orderly columns of numbers than mysteries of the paranormal.

"What happened?" I pressed. "Tell me about it."

But Betsy couldn't. Rita had not told her any more.

"And I didn't want to call on the phone and upset Mom so I wondered if you could go up and talk to her in person."

I certainly could, and the next week found me in Mother's little house on the farm.

"Mom," I asked, after she had pulled out the cookies, lined up the magazines she wanted me to take home and checked on all the kids, "what's this about you seeing a spirit or something?"

Instantly her face clouded. Her whole body stilled and shrank down as if preparing to leap a great chasm. Turning from the sink, she looked me square in the eye. I waited, knowing she was considering in her own mind my sincerity and need for knowing. Then she walked over to the table, picked up the place mat and sat down.

I expected questionings or vague allusions to the strange visitor, instead she started right in without another word, surprising me with her precise dictation, almost as if it had been carefully written out and memorized. I grabbed a pen and took notes to get it right, not knowing her story would tell me of what could only be, judging from my experience with similar stories of such vividness and clarity, a visit from an angel of God.

"I went to bed and was really tired," she said. "I fell asleep immediately. It was one or one thirty when I was awakened suddenly. I always wear my wristwatch to bed, because I don't have a clock I can read in the dark. I can't remember just how I woke up, but when I did I was looking at this person."

A person, standing by her bed? Mother has seen scarecrows in gardens, people dressed up in costumes, and almost every kind of doll in the world, so when she said "person," I knew this apparition had to be real.

"He, I say it was a he because his features were kind of heavy," she explained, "he had rather large brown eyes and his hair was pulled back and then twisted into a knot. He had . . ." she paused. "I immediately thought about the bones of African nations, that held his hair back, and his hair was dishwater blond."

Ah. That particular color of dull brown with just enough highlights to bring it over to a passable shade of light gold, which Mother always identified, rather scornfully, as "dishwater."

"There was light in my room, and I don't know where it came from, because I didn't have my light on. I don't know if there were any other people in the room, although it felt like there was," she continued.

"This person looked straight at my eyes, with no expression change in his face. He didn't look mad or unhappy or anything like that. He had a good expression on his face.

"Then I realized I was holding my hands against my chest, so tight that it could cause a muscle cramp. I thought, *You could have a heart attack right here and no one would know it was because of the Spirit.*

"I was still looking at him, and he at me. He was 7 ½ feet tall, taller than the people I know." And the children in our family range in the upper scale with most of us girls being almost six feet tall and the boys nearer six feet plus inches.

"He wore a tunic," she went on, "the shirt came down to the calves of his legs and it was a foam green."

Foam green? I looked up from my writing. A soft-muted cross between turquoise and light green, it literally looks like the breakers on the ocean. Quite uncommon, foam green is rarely seen except in summer cottons and the occasional quilt pattern. But Mother could definitely identify that particular shade of color from all of her years working with fabric.

"And then there was another jacket to the tunic," she said. "I don't know if there was a belt, it was pulled around so it met in the front and came down to his knees. It looked like it was expensive," she added, she who has sewn everything from blue denim to velvet. "It had a band around the shirt and up the jacket, woven silk, its weave set it aside so you would immediately notice it."

All of the details matched what would be called a tunic today. Expensive fabric. Silk, woven so beautifully it drew the eye to the intricate design, banded at the hem and fronts of the jacket. And Mother instinctively knew there was supposed to be a belt, for that is what was worn with them.

Tunics were an ancient dress, suited to Greek and Roman times, a simple slip-on garment with no collar, whose length extended to the knees or below. A jacket, made of the same material, was usually sewn to wear over the top. Lustrous bands of a complementary color often encircled the hem of the tunic and sleeves, or as in Mother's case, set off the fronts of the jacket.

"He had a tablet in his hands and a pencil in his hand," she went on. "He never moved, but you couldn't say he was a stick man or anything like that. He was a living, breathing person." Of that she was sure.

"His feet were hidden by my bed so I couldn't see his shoes," she added. I almost chuckled to think of Mother trying to peer over the side of the mattress to check out his feet. But after the glorious tunic, wouldn't you want to see the rich leather sandals with straps wrapped around his ankles, or was he barefoot? For that is another sign of angels, that they often appear without shoes. Was Mother looking for this confirmation of him coming from heaven?

"He was still watching me, and I, him," she said. "I thought, *If I can get to the telephone and call Boone to come over,* and I turned, and came back to my original position and he was gone."

Silence. She waited a bit, then added. "The light was gone."

"Of course I didn't go to sleep for about two hours. I just wondered why he was there and why he looked at me the whole time. I wasn't really frightened, but was worn out by it. It bothered me to the extent that I asked God to prevent him from coming again.

"But four nights later, the same thing happened," she sighed. "The same vision, same light, and he looked at me about the same amount of time. I woke up and was startled, and I didn't even intend to use the telephone, the second time. I didn't think it would make any difference.

"I feel if I had tried to speak or turned away, he would have looked away, but he never batted his eyelashes, never turned his head, and then he was gone." She took a deep breath and lifted her left arm to rest it on the table.

"Mom," I asked, "why do you call him a Spirit?"

"Well," she pondered, "he came with no noise, he didn't speak and he left in the same manner. I wasn't frightened or anything. I felt good while he was there. But," she added, leaning against the back of the chair, "it's been a relief to me that he has not come back."

Mother never spoke of her unexpected visitor again, while I returned home to ponder the mystery of it. In the Bible, angels are spoken of as spirits. *Are they not all ministering spirits, sent forth to minister for them who shall be heirs of salvation? Hebrews 1:14* And yet, this Spirit did not seem to be ministering to her in any way.

Was there a preacher in Mother's younger years who referred to them so? Did her own mother call them such? Is there an Angel of the Books in heaven, whose one task is to keep a log, marking down each soul, their time of sojourn on the earth and date of return? Was Mother nearing her end? Did the angel come to prepare her? Or could he have been simply her guardian angel, come to check on her and make sure she was all right? I do not know.

I later wondered, however, if it was a coincidence when I saw the photograph of an old old painting of three glorious angels, each dressed in an exquisite brocade tunic with—you guessed it—golden bands encircling the hem and sleeves, and I immediately thought of Mother and her extraordinary Spirit.

TALAYE

I s it written, that in order to be validated, angels must be seen with the human eye? Can they not appear while we sleep, in dreams or visions, and be just as real as when they come before us in wakefulness?

Joseph, fiancé of Mary, obviously did not believe her story of angelic visitation, and had to be confronted with God's messenger, through a dream, before he consented to marry her as planned.

What was there in Joseph's encounter, which so easily could have been discounted as nothing more than a dream, that caused him to accept the words of the angel?

> *Joseph, thou son of David, fear not to take unto thee Mary thy wife: for that which is conceived in her is of the Holy Ghost. And she shall bring forth a son, and thou shalt call his name JESUS: for he shall save his people from their sins.* Matthew 1:20–21

Apparently, after scoffing at Mary and her preposterous tale of the angel Gabriel coming to her and telling her she would bear the child, Jesus, the Son of the Highest, Joseph quickly snapped to attention when the glory and majesty of God's own angel stood before *him*, to the point of making sure the Holy Child was named as the angel directed, *JESUS*, when He was born all those months later in Bethlehem.

Three times more, at critical moments in their new marriage, God spoke to Joseph through an angel in a dream, sending commands which it is interesting to note, are always instantly obeyed. Joseph must have gotten the message. Never again does he question either God or the angels.

The first directive comes after the departure of the wise men, who themselves were warned by God in a dream to circumvent King Herod, who had sought to deceive the wise men by asking them to return and tell him where the child was located so that he might go and worship him also. Heeding God's instruction, the wise men ignored the crafty Herod and left Bethlehem by a route bypassing Jerusalem.

When the wise men had safely gone, the angel of the Lord came to Joseph again while he slept, telling him to take Mary and Jesus and flee into Egypt.

This must have seemed odd to Joseph, but he never questioned the strange order, waking at once to rouse Mary and prepare for flight. I can imagine the confusion of Mary as she struggled to understand why her husband was hurrying them out in the middle of the night.

"But Joseph," she questions. "Can't we wait until morning?"

"No!" he says. "The angel said 'Get up and go.'" Or more specifically,

Arise, and take the young child and his mother, and flee into Egypt, and be thou there until I bring thee word: for Herod will seek the young child to destroy him. Matthew 2:13

Flee means 'go at once'; it does not suggest any waiting around, so they left, with only the stars to guide them, ironically seeking safety in the very country that Moses had fled in order to save the Jews. Until the death of Herod, Joseph and Mary sheltered the young child in Egypt, and when the Roman king no longer lived, knowing now that the danger to Jesus had passed, God once again sent His emissary to speak to Joseph in a dream, assuring him they could return to their homeland in safety by saying:

Arise, and take the young child and his mother, and go into the land of Israel: for they are dead which sought the young child's life. Matthew 2:20

Joseph obediently packs up Mary and Jesus and treks back to Israel, but God has one more dispatch for him, courtesy of the angel. To beware of the son of Herod, Archelaus. As blood thirsty as Herod, Archelaus killed at will. When

Joseph learned that he ruled Judea in his father's place, he was afraid Archelaus would also seek to murder Jesus.

Joseph's fears were well founded, because for the third and last time, God warned Joseph in a dream, to stay away from Archelaus. Joseph listened. But the only way to do so was to live outside of the jurisdiction of Judea. So instead of returning to the land of his fathers and settling in Bethlehem or Jerusalem, Joseph traveled on to Galilee to dwell in the city of Nazareth. There is never a question of Joseph doubting the angel from the first time he sees him in the dream.

And so it was with Talaye.

For six months, our writer's group in Circle had been preparing for the coming of three "Tumblewords" writers, published authors who were going to speak in our town through a grant provided by the Montana Arts Council. We had chosen a poet, a novelist, and an essayist, each to arrive in a different month throughout the winter.

I was scheduled to greet our first author, David Cates from Missoula, but was unable to do so as a cow and I had battled, and she won. Instead of attending the program, I lay on the couch with my leg in the air and a very badly sprained ankle swollen to twice its size.

Two months' healing found me welcoming our second guest instead, Lowell Jaeger, a poet from Big Fork who also taught writing at Flathead Valley Community College in Kalispell. Amongst the books and miniature tables of the grade school library, he showed the youngsters how to see first with their hearts and then in their minds, as they placed snippets of life into meters that rhymed, or not. Their very own poems.

For his second class, we walked over to the high school where I left him with the freshmen, returning at noon to take him to lunch in the school's cafeteria. Visiting with the ease of an instructor who regularly greets students and makes them friends, Lowell quizzed me over lasagna and hot garlic bread.

"How long have you lived in Circle? Do you have a family? What do you like to read? Fiction? Non-fiction? Why?" and when I reluctantly admitted I could not stand most fiction because the stories were so . . . *fakey,* he stopped, looked me directly in the eyes, and said, "Ah-h-h, that's because you are a writer."

Who is this person that in ten minutes has discovered the core of my being? I *am* a writer; he doesn't know it, (or does he?). I've written columns, magazine articles, and am now working on a book. It's a rather unusual one in that it has no plot, no time line or characters I've constructed, but instead is composed entirely of stories that come to me unbidden, at most unusual times, and while I have the beginning, I have no idea of what the end shall be. My book of angels.

Should I tell him? Across the laminate top of the lunchroom table, I study his face. Open, quiet, honest. A teacher, who has stayed up nights writing his own poems. A writer, who has held in his hands the books with his name on the cover. Someone I felt sure would not criticize or ridicule this attempt of mine.

"I *am* working on a book," I decide, "about people who have seen angels."

"Angels!" he exclaimed. "Then you must talk to my daughter, Talaye. She had a dream about angels."

And just like that, another story was given me.

A week later, Lowell called and introduced me to his daughter.

"Talaye is a beautiful girl, old beyond her years and full of quiet wisdom," he said. "We are lucky to have her." I did not know at the time that she had been very ill as an infant and nearly died.

"Talaye," he continued, as she picked up the other phone, "this is the lady I told you about who is writing a book on angels." She was reserved, hesitant almost, a fifteen-year-old sophomore in high school that January of 1994, not sure of what she could tell this person without being laughed at, but as we talked, she relaxed and began to relate her experience to me.

Oddly, in her dream she had been sleeping. And woke up to get ready for school.

"In my dream, I went outside to start my car, I tried and tried but it wouldn't start," she said, "so I got on my bike and rode to my friend's house to get her to go to school with me."

As happens so many times in dreams, circumstances changed instantly and without reason. "Suddenly we started running," she explained, "just running and running and running, like down a road, and we came to the end of the road.

"It was like it dropped off, and you could see the world. We looked down and we could see the Earth."

How strange it must have been for those two girls, to peer over the edge of a towering cliff and sight our planet Earth, hanging out in space, far away.

"I knew I had to go to it," she continued, the fear of this requirement surfacing in the slight trembling of her voice. "I had to jump down to it."

She paused, then admitted, "I was kind of scared, but I said, 'I've got to do this.'"

And the moment she decided, help appeared.

"Then a guy came. He said to me, 'I've been sent down here because we don't want you to do this alone.' He took my hand, my right hand I think, and we kind of jumped down to the world. I felt real comfortable with him. Real safe." Great relief floods her voice as she added. "I was really glad he was there."

"What did this fellow look like?" I asked.

"He had light brown hair, with really blue eyes," she answered.

"Did you think he was Jesus?"

"No," she said immediately. "I thought he was an angel."

"Didn't you think there was more than one angel?" asked her father.

"Yes," said Talaye. "There was one for my friend, I didn't see him really good, I remember seeing him out of the corner of my eye."

So there were two, one for each of the girls. Their guardian angel assisting them on the journey from the far reaches of heaven to our earthly home.

"What did you think about this dream, Talaye?" I asked.

You could see her smiling over the phone. "I thought it was really neat," she responded. "Pretty powerful."

"Why don't you tell her about your other experience?" suggested Lowell quietly.

"There's more?"

"Yes. It happened in Iowa when I was six or seven. I woke up one morning and it was like I was half awake. I got out of bed and started walking, going down the stairs. Suddenly I felt myself floating, I just floated down and was put down at the bottom."

Put down. Those are words a person uses when they have been picked up.

"Are you sure you were *carried* down the steps, that it wasn't a dream?" I asked.

"No, I could feel my feet," she said firmly. "I was really tired but I knew I didn't touch the stairs. I went all the way, fifteen steps, and was left standing at the bottom."

A sort of bewilderment swept through me. How could that have happened? There had to be someone bigger than her, strong and tall that could carry her while still navigating the steps.

Was it the same angel who came with her to earth? Did he lovingly pick her up to keep her from falling? Was he afraid she might stumble and hurt herself? And is he protecting her yet today, just as he did in her dream on the way to our earth?

Who is to know? Certainly not I, but perhaps the angel who spoke to Joseph so long ago could tell us all.

GRANDMA STRUTZ

No matter how hard I tried, Grandma Strutz eluded me. You would think that after being miraculously healed in a hospital, everyone around her would have some of her story to tell. They didn't. And neither did she.

The matriarch of her family, she resided in a nursing home in Billings, although at ninety-six, her mind was as sharp and clear as a girl's of twenty. Everyone called her Grandma Strutz, although we weren't related to her.

"Grandma," I asked, after receiving permission from her son to call, "would you tell me about your angel?"

"No," she responded in a delicate aged voice that fell off over the line, but in which I recognized the steel of surviving childhood without a mother and successfully enduring all the days of the Great Depression. "I do not want to talk about it."

How could anyone not be willing to discuss the most incredible experience of their life? One which baffled every person who heard it, thrilling some with its impossibilities while causing others to be struck dumbfounded in disbelief? Especially when it concerned the workings of heaven. She who had been the wife of a minister all of her life, who surely had heard of miracles, possibly seen them. Had prayed and listened to prayers countless times. Knew the Lord Jesus loved his children and sent help for them, help which often confounded us, we who are given only human capabilities. Was she afraid of me? Distrustful? Maybe so. And for that I could not blame her. She had after all, seen many years, and in them probably every kind of person. How was she to know who I was?

Perhaps if I just asked again. Which I did. More than once. To which she declined again, quietly but determined, and I knew if I asked a thousand times, her answer would be the same.

What does one do when you cannot get the information you need from the source, the spring of living water? You dip your cup into the rivulets which flow from it. So I began a campaign of ripples; asking at the hospital where she was cared for, the doctor who treated her, a nurse who remembered the case but could not recall the specifics of her healing, another who agreed to check with others and post a request for me on the bulletin board.

Each inquiry fell flat, while my hope deflated like an inner tube losing air. I looked for cooks, janitors, aides, anyone at the hospital who may have talked to her, and searched for the person who had been so astonished at hearing the story, how the angel came and healed her, that they became a Christian at her bedside.

But like that messenger who appeared and then vanished

from sight, all those souls seemed to have dissipated into a retreating mist, tantalizing me with an authenticity which could not be proven. So I decided to go back to the beginning, and tell it the way I'd heard it.

On a cold October day in 1993, Milton and I stopped on the way home from Miles City, Montana to pay our friends for the seed wheat we had bought from them that fall.

Rain had been falling all afternoon, a cold miserable sleet which turned to ice as the temperature dropped. Everything in our view sagged with the heavy burden of its weight. Fences, trees, long power lines. Anything that could catch the water and hold it. Even the grass was coated, crunching like brittle stalks of glass beneath our feet as we pulled up to the house and stepped from the pickup.

Our friends Myron and Polly were distraught in the kitchen, waiting for the cottonwoods they had tended to fall. Sharp cracks exploded like gunshots as branches snapped and clattered to the ground, hung with ice-coated leaves they could no longer hold. We rushed to the window to determine which ones had broken, and tried to console each other over their loss. Trees in eastern Montana are precious. And the ones planted around homes are treated like children. I hated to think of all the years spent hoeing, watering, and building fence around them to keep rabbits and varmints from killing them, only to have them decimated by layers of frozen ice.

I attempted to distract Polly by chattering, while she insisted upon serving us supper amongst the chaos. What could I do to help her? How could I take her mind off the terrible storm? Suddenly I remembered my angels.

"Polly," I questioned at her stove. "Do you know of anyone who has seen an angel?"

"Angels!" exclaimed Myron. "You need to talk to Grandma Strutz. *She* has a story for you." And he hurried to dig up Grandma Strutz's son's name and give it to me.

"Here," he said, handing me a bit of white paper with a phone number written on it. "Call Bob and he will tell you all about it."

And so I did.

When she was just six years old, Grandma Strutz's mother died, leaving her to be raised in foster homes in South Dakota and Wisconsin. Perhaps it was this loss which cemented her strength of will and taught her to think for herself.

Although left without any immediate family, an aunt intervened when she became old enough to learn a trade, urging her to become a nurse, an acceptable vocation for young women in the 1920s.

She agreed, attending nurse's college, and took a job in the Bismarck, North Dakota, hospital after graduation. There she showed both skill and compassion in caring for her patients, and was quickly promoted to Head Surgical

Nurse, a position which demanded extreme competence, and trust by the surgeons.

At this time she became engaged to the man she would marry, but the sermons of a traveling evangelist swept her out of the operating room and into the front parlor of a manse when her fiancé was so affected by this minister's dynamic preaching that he determined to become one himself.

Thus it was that Grandma Strutz became a pastor's wife, raising their three children while dispensing kindness and caring to the congregations they led, as she had earlier done in the hospital wards.

That she ever thought of seeing an angel, no one knows. Certainly she believed in them, for a strong faith in God was the bedrock of her life. Nothing shook that. Not the eventual loss of her husband or the passing of years that lengthened into nearly a century of living.

Not even heart attacks, the first of which struck her at the age of ninety-two. Like earthquakes which appear to do little damage, it receded, leaving no after effects. The second tried to kill her. For several days, Grandma Strutz lay in a coma, a silent patient in a hospital bed, like so many she had tended in her nursing days, unable to speak, move or hear, knowing neither her children or the efforts of the medical staff to save her. When the doctor at last gave up hope, he informed her family she would not live. How could they know that when they left the hospital to make arrangements for her funeral, God was preparing a miracle for the mother they loved.

For what none of them realized, was that while Rosalie Strutz may not have been able to communicate with her family, she could still talk to God. While her weakened body struggled behind the oxygen mask to pull in every breath, her mind called out to her heavenly Father.

Lord! she cried, with all the visitors gone, the hush of the hospital at night around her. *I am just existing, and I'll stay as long as you want me to, but I haven't been able to do anything, not even lift a chair. Lord, if it's your will, help me.*

And the angel came. She, lucid, totally rational in thought, saw him standing by her bed and recognized him immediately as being sent from God. He spoke to her distinctly, plainly.

"It is not time for you to go."

"But I'm ready to go," she countered, slightly querulous. Who would not be with ninety some years of living behind them, their heart struggling with every beat to send the blood on its way, stop, rest an instant and then beat again?

"Take up your bed and walk," the angel commanded. She stared at him, incredulous. What was this he expected? For her to *walk*? To stand, on legs with no strength? How could it be done? But where had she heard that before? More than once. Instructions from her Saviour. To the man at the pool. The man with the palsy. The same words to men sick, incapacitated, just as she was now.

Take up thy bed, and walk. John 5:8; Mark 2:9

Perhaps a small door opened, and Grandma Strutz remembered that long ago verse. And the immediate action of the men. How they obeyed the Christ. Believing what He could do. That He could heal them.

In one swift movement, she cast off the covers and threw her legs over the bed. Jumping up, she grabbed a chair, thrust it out of the way and without a moment's hesitation, walked out the door and down the hall.

"Rosalie!" The nurses on duty gaped in fear, for not one had seen her out of the bed since she'd arrived. Ignoring them, Grandma Strutz strode to the north end of the hallway, turned around and walked back to her room. She was following the orders of a Higher Power, brought by a messenger only she could see. No earthly creature would dissuade her.

When the doctor arrived, hastily summoned by the nurses, she was standing at the sink with her back to him. "Rosalie," he asked tentatively, "is that you?"

Turning to him smiling, she nodded and said, "Yes," standing as strong and straight as if she were fifty years younger. From a dying woman, whose casket had already been chosen, to the bright, energetic person she was before her heart attacks, Grandma Strutz had been returned to a healthy active life, healed in a twinkling by a mysterious angel who disappeared as quickly as he had come. Mission accomplished.

Praise be to God.

BETSY

Milton and I pulled into the yard just before dark after spending the day visiting Mom at the nursing home in Miles City. I walked into the kitchen, automatically glancing at the answering machine as I piled sacks of groceries on the counter beside the phone. Four messages blinked at me. *That's odd.* Sometimes two or three people will call when we're away, but usually no more. The slightest niggling of alarm caught the edge of my consciousness as an uncontrollable shiver ran across my arms. *What's going on here?* I wondered, instantly alert to a danger I could not see. Laying my coat on the tall stool beneath the island I turned and punched the button marked *Play.*

"Wanda," my big sister's voice, startling me with its frailness, barely whispered from the tape. I leaned closer, as if nearness would infuse her with strength, straining to catch the almost inaudible words. "Call me . . . I'm in the hospital . . . please call."

Icicles prickled my scalp. *What's wrong? Why is Betsy in the hospital?*

Click! Number Two. The tape switched over to her

husband Wayne, whose normally self-confident voice now sounded worried and drained.

"Wanda, this is Wayne. Betsy's having heart surgery. Call my cell as soon as you can."

Dear God.

I froze by the phone, swept back to the kitchen in Grandpa's log house forty-five years before, noisy with the clang of dish pans and children's laughter as we finished up supper and got the dishes done. All that suddenly silenced by a knock on the door and mother sagging ashen against the wall.

Daddy. Nearly dead of a heart attack a hundred and fifty miles away.

Click! The answering machine severed the memory, yanked me back to the next call. Rhonda, Betsy's daughter.

"Wanda, Tammie and I are on our way to Reno. Please call my cell phone."

Seeing me hunched over the phone, Milton stopped in the doorway to the kitchen as he brought in another armful of groceries.

"What's going on?" he asked, looking puzzled. Without thinking, my hand flew up, palm out in the ages old signal to Stop. Listen. Afraid he would keep talking and I would miss the last message as the number flipped over.

"Wandie!" Mary Ann's voice jumped out. "Betsy is in Reno, she's having heart surgery, please call me when you get home."

A dreadful fear like lead settled in my stomach.

Veins. Hearts. The curse of our family. They hide, seemingly well beneath muscle and bone, until disaster, an explosion of blood driven through a ruptured blood vessel, or a clog locking up an artery, strikes one of us down.

How many had there been? Grandma Whitmer, stepping off the train in Chickasha, Oklahoma, to collapse on the platform and die in the arms of her son. Heart attack.

Mother's mom, paralyzed from a clot released during the manipulations of a chiropractor, falling to the sidewalk as she left the office, never to walk again.

Daddy, operated on for an aneurysm near his heart, both mother and his doctors were so pleased with his recovery that she left Minneapolis to come back to Montana, barely reaching home before his death.

Mother herself, felled by an aneurysm in the brain, only the grace of God saving her life. The doctors, having given her a one percent chance to live, called it a miracle, watching in amazement as she healed with the total use of her arms and legs and spoke with free unfettered speech.

And now my sister Betsy, in Reno with heart surgery, the same age Mom had been when her aneurysm burst, fifty-nine years old. I picked up the phone and started dialing.

None of us in Montana, a thousand miles away from Elko, Nevada, knew what was happening that morning of February 15, 2005. Betsy awoke early, with an excruciating pain piercing her back, so terrible she could hardly breathe.

"It felt like someone was trying to ram a two by four between my shoulder blades," she told me later. "I could hardly move, and when I tried to get out of bed, it was like my legs were frozen. I thought, *I am going to die, right here and now.* Because I'd read about women having pain in their shoulders and it was heart problems.

"I tried to roll over on my left arm, with my elbow supporting me and the pain was unbelievable. That's when I knew I was in serious trouble. I forced myself to get up and walk to reach the bathroom, but I was really fearful of falling and could only move like a tin soldier, with my legs stiff and outward. I hung onto the door facings and started hollering for Wayne. He takes his hearing aids out when he sleeps at night so I knew he could not hear me.

"By the time I got to our bedroom door, he had started to wake up. I took two big steps and collapsed at the foot of the bed. He said, 'Honey, what's the matter?' Later he told me I was the color of paste.

"'You have to get me to the hospital *now*,' I said. 'I think I'm having a heart attack.'

"He got right up and rushed around getting me dressed and the van warmed up. It was bitterly cold out, with fog, and he thought about calling 911, but knew he could get to the hospital faster than the ambulance because we're only six miles away."

As they went out the door, Betsy caught sight of the clock. It read 7:37 am. *Why am I remembering this?* she wondered, not knowing the ticking of her life now came down to minutes, for the inner lining of her aorta had split open, a tear like a scissors' snip, but deadly dangerous, because every beat of her heart now pushed blood against it, forcing the lining away from the outside membrane, collapsing it inside the vessel and pushing it down towards the aortic branch above the kidneys. When the torn lining reached that junction, no doctor on earth could save her.

None of this I knew yet, as I waited for Wayne's cell phone to ring. The instant he answered, I burst out.

"What's happening, Wayne?"

"Betsy has a descending aorta," he said, his voice reeling from shock.

Aneurysms I understood. A "descending aorta" I'd never heard of.

"What's that, an aneurysm?"

"No, it's different," he explained. "The lining has torn. It's falling down inside the vein. They have to take it out."

Take it out! How in the world do you replace a part of the aorta and still live?

"How can they do that? Do they use another vein?"

"It's a fabric, material the body doesn't reject. Like a synthetic vein."

I started to shake, the phone banging against my ear as I remembered operations, my family in hospitals. Wanting to scream the questions I could not ask, the only ones that mattered. *Is she going to live? Will she die?*

Dear God. A desperate petition rose from my heart. *Please God. Don't let her die. Please God, angels around her. The right doctors. Guide their hands. Do what needs to be done. Don't let her die. Please God, keep her alive.* And suddenly realized I did not even know where they were.

"Where are you, Wayne?" I tried to keep the terror in my voice from showing, acting as if I was unperturbed, not dropped to my knees before the throne of God, begging like a tramp in rags.

"Washoe Med. In Reno."

"How did you get there?"

"We flew. On air ambulance."

And in an instant, I remembered twenty-two years before, watching for the light, a clear green strobe in the black of night, affixed to the belly of the plane taking my mother from Wolf Point, Montana to Billings, three hundred miles away, when she also lay on the pillow of death. Milton and I racing behind in the car, silent, only the sound of the engine between us, the cold glass of the window pressed against my face as I strained to pick up every emerald flash in the southwestern sky. Praying then too. *Please God. Keep Mother alive.*

But in Betsy's hometown of Elko, there were no planes waiting when Wayne slid up to the emergency room door. Inside, the day shift was just coming on. As switchboard operator at the hospital, Betsy knew every person who worked there and the position they held. Later, she told me what had happened.

"The receptionist saw me and said 'Betsy, what are you doing here?' in a *Good Morning* friendly kind of voice.

"'I think I'm having a heart attack,' Betsy said, and she started pulling my files as fast as she could. They got me to the triage center right away and I was just about out—for good. Dr. Stefanko came in immediately and started evaluations. He thought it was a blood clot in my lungs but there was nothing there, then he drew blood to check for a heart attack, and it wasn't that.

"They rushed me to the CAT scan and there it was, big as life, tearing and taking my life with every inch it went. Dr. Stefanko immediately called my regular doctor, Dr. Whimple, and told him the findings and that he was going to transport me out.

"I could hear voices at my head but no bodies to go with them. I remember a lady saying, 'Betsy, where do you want to go, Salt Lake City or Reno?' and both Wayne and I said at the same time, 'Reno. Washoe Med.' And I thought, *Oh, my God. The only time they ship you on the airplane is when you're dying.*

"Everyone in ER was in shock. I was just about dead and they all knew it. As they were wheeling me out to the ambulance, the nurse told the crew when I came in I had non-life supporting vitals. Dr. Stefanko was standing at my feet giving orders, looking as white as a sheet. He was very sober faced, sad, and scared."

Because he knew the statistics for her condition. Ninety percent of patients with descending aortas die. An hour to surgery was twice too long. And that was the length of the flight to Reno. Knowing she could very possibly die en route, he gave Wayne permission to fly with her and handed him the results of the CAT scan, on the slender chance that she would still be alive when they reached the hospital.

Wayne squeezed into the tiny cockpit while the med flight crew got Betsy on board. "Keep it low and fast," the nurse told the pilot, as they taxied onto the strip and up into the sky, headed west.

"I felt like I was on the cotton speedway," said Betsy, "the sun so bright, shining on the white clouds. Out the window, at my left shoulder, I could see this little angel on the wing of the plane. It was just a glimmer, at the very end of the wing, like an extra "bump" on the tip, nothing I had ever seen before flying commercial flights, and I *knew* it was an angel. It was somehow more powerful and majestic, something that was carrying me right on *top* of it, like it was hugging me and making sure I wouldn't fall. It was the only time I was not in pain, and lasted through the whole flight.

"I looked out and I saw the plane flying through the air, as if I was watching it from a distance." And right then she knew. She was dying, her spirit starting its journey back home. A great remorse swelled up inside her as she thought of Mother so far away in Montana. Being told in the nursing home that her eldest daughter had died. Knowing what grief it would bring her. Betsy could hardly stand the thought.

Please don't let me die, she prayed. *I can't go before Mom, it would kill her, I can't die now.* And with that last request, peace came. The next thing she knew they were circling to land.

"There was a problem at the airport," Betsy recalled, "and the pilot said, 'I'm going to put it down the first time.' He knew there was no time to go around again and he landed as smooth as can be. Fifty-five minutes to Reno," she said, "and the pain began again and never stopped."

The heart surgeon Dr. Stefanko wanted in Reno happened to be on call at Washoe Med that morning. Hastily, he'd assembled the operating crew and was waiting when the ambulance spun up to the ER carrying Betsy, sirens wailing. Sticking the images from the CAT scan onto the light box, he noted their poor quality and sharply asked. "Where did that scan come from?"

"I hand carried it from Elko," said Wayne.

"Well, it's not very good, but we don't have time to do it over," the doctor said. "This woman has got to go into surgery right now."

"They had me on the gurney, running down the hall, while the pain was getting worse," said Betsy, "and all I could think about was Mom, twenty-four years ago with her brain aneurysm and I felt so terrible for her."

In Miles City, Mother had woken up that very night. This in itself was not unusual, because as she grew older, it seemed she rarely slept the night through. She lay awake for a moment, listening to the sounds of the nursing home around her, footsteps hurrying down the hall, the creak of a door opening, noises that intruded upon the peace of her sleep, but which she had come to accept.

Shifting under the covers, she turned her head and saw someone she did not recognize. A little girl, standing silently beside the sewing machine table where Mother worked every day on her quilts. Children rarely came to the nursing home, and most assuredly never into her room during the night. Especially alone.

Mother sat up in bed, and speaking quietly so that she would not scare her, asked the child. "What are you doing here?"

The little girl flinched, which told Mother she had heard the question but refused to answer it. All of the child's attention was focused on the sewing machine where her little fingers were fooling with something that Mother could not see.

"Can I help you?" Mother said, noticing her long, blondish red hair which curled down to her shoulders. Suddenly Mother realized that though the room was dark, she could see the child perfectly well, just as if it were plain day. About four or five years old, she was dressed in a pretty spring dress, sleeveless and ruffly with the skirt falling below her knees.

Getting up off the bed, Mother reached out to touch the child on her shoulder and immediately the little girl turned away from her and vanished. She did not move, take a step or walk out the door. She simply disappeared, poof! in an instant, from right in front of Mother's eyes, as if she had never been there. The child was gone.

Sinking back onto the bed, a heavy foreboding filled Mother's heart. This was an angel. An angel with a mission. To deliver a message.

Something is happening to one of my daughters, she thought. Swiftly she went through us six girls, where we were, what we were doing. Betsy was at home in Elko, fine as far as she knew. Patsy in Yakima. Mary Ann was working at the school in Grass Range. Rita stopped by every day from her job in Miles City. Wanda was on the farm, watching over the cows. Barbara had her job in Canada. Could there have been a car wreck, an accident? Were any flying, could one have been injured? Until she learned otherwise, there was only one thing she could do. Mother leaned back against the pillows and started praying.

The next day, the fifteenth of February, my twin, Rita, and I both came to see her. That took two off the list. No phone calls, no reports from hospitals or distraught husbands, but the worry persisted. Who could it be, and what was happening?

The answer to her questions came when I called her that evening to tell her Betsy had nearly died and was in the hospital in Reno following heart surgery. Mother's calmness and acceptance of the serious operation surprised me until she said.

"A little girl angel came last night to warn me that one of my daughters was in trouble."

A child who should not have been there, *could* not have been, but was. Who came in silence, spoke not a word and disappeared in a flash, as soon as her errand was complete. Leaving Mother to pray for the safety of her daughters, even as Betsy hung in the void between life and death. Each thinking of the other.

Did that forewarning tip the scales for Betsy? Did Mother's call for help cause God to send her the angel on the airplane's wing, the one which held her and kept her alive on the long flight to Reno? Did it keep the lining in her aorta from falling, so that she had time to reach the hospital and the skillful surgeon who saved her life? Did it stop the clock?

We will forever wonder, being sure of only one thing. Betsy lives. And it was a miracle. Every doctor says so.

MARY ANNE

I pushed open the door of the post office, nearly running over my friend, June, and her daughter, Jenny, standing beside her. Smart, petite, and beautiful, Jenny had graduated from high school with our son, Ross, and determined to become a doctor. For over ten years she'd toiled, refusing to give up when it could have been easy to do so, and finally achieved her MD. Just the week before, there'd been an article in the local paper telling about the trip she took to Nepal on a medical rotation with other American doctors, to care for the children of that country.

Surprised and delighted to see her, I bent down to give her a big hug, congratulating her on becoming a doctor. Her face beamed, pride and jubilation each trying to outdo the other. A beautiful cashmere scarf wrapped around the collar of her coat against the December chill.

"Are these the scarves you're selling for the orphans in Nepal?" I asked, remembering the story she'd told of the children in the newspaper.

"Yes," she nodded, running the long fringe through her fingers as her eyes darkened, "to try and get the kids off the streets."

Amazingly, while in Nepal she'd met a young man from Montana who had started an orphanage in Nepal for homeless children. Shocked when he realized the youngsters were being drawn into the underground and targeted for trafficking in the vile slavery and sex trades across Asia, he'd taken it upon himself to set up a home for them where they could be safe.

Not wishing to ask for donations to keep his orphanage going, he had decided to sell native cashmere scarves to help fund its operation. Jenny's heart went out to those homeless children, and she had mentioned his work in her newspaper story about going to Nepal.

A tiny germ of an idea flickered in my brain. Maybe this was something an inspirational magazine would be interested in. "Is John a Christian?" I asked.

"Oh, yes! Very much so."

"Maybe I should ask if I could do a story about him."

"Call—or email him," she said. "I'm sure he would."

That night, I dug out the article again and read it through. *What do you think, God? Should I ask John for a story about the orphans in Nepal?*

Yes, the answer came softly, *and ask him if he's ever seen an angel.*

An angel? What did that have to do with the children? It seemed strange, but if anything, I've learned that God does not operate the way we do, so I took his suggestion and tacked it on to the end of my email. To my surprise, John answered back immediately, with information that caused me to once again smile at God's nudgings.

"I myself have never seen one that I know of," he replied, "but my mom did."

Now I knew why I'd run into Jenny in the post office. And why I was supposed to ask John about the angels. Because God had another story waiting for me.

Contented was perhaps a good word to describe John's mother, Mary Anne, that early spring day. John had just left for a ski trip at Grand Targhee, Idaho, with two of his friends and their parents over spring break, her husband was happily playing golf, and Easter was just three days away. How could life be any better?

Skiing was something the whole family loved. Surrounded by the Rocky Mountains around their home in Helena, Montana, winter time put them right in the middle of some of the best ski runs in the West. John was just a little guy, only three years old when his parents put him on skis for the first time, and he'd zipped down the slopes ever since. Now a freshman in high school, he had grown to a good height at five feet ten inches tall, and become an excellent skier to boot. A new pair of ski poles that he'd just bought was tucked into his bag to take on this much antici-pated trip with his classmates.

As soon as the boys got to Grand Targhee, they grabbed the lift to the top, eager to jump into the fresh powder covering the mountain. Dropping off the chairs, they left the groomed trails to weave through the snow-laden trees. Swift and agile, John timed his turns with instinct and accuracy, pivoting around the poles in his hands to turn with deliberate precision, skiing a symphony as skilled and graceful as a ballet dancer on stage.

Left. Right. Whistling through the pristine air of the high Rockies, filled with exhilaration at the beauty and grandeur of the magnificent Tetons rising at his back, John's spirit rose in joy and delight as he navigated a fresh track down the welcoming slopes. Crystals of powder flying in his face, he stuck his new pole into the snow to swing around a tree, swooped past its evergreen boughs, shifted weight, thrust again . . . and felt a lurch as the pole plunged downward unchecked, the basket broken loose from its tubing, pulling him off balance, flinging him straight into a tree.

So fast, it could not be stopped. So hard, John's head slammed into the tree trunk sounding like a rifle shot exploding in the thin air. Ka-boom! The force of the blow piled him up under the branches in a crumpled heap of stillness.

"John!" His high school buddy watched in horror as he lay sprawled on the snow unconscious, skis strapped on flailing legs as instant grand mal seizures shook his body like a broken puppet. *Oh my God. He's dying. John's dying.*

"I've got to get help!" Pushing off, his friend shot down the slope frantically searching for his parents and the ski patrol.

The first phone call said he was ok. "They called from a little clinic where they'd taken him," said Mary Anne. "They thought he'd probably had a concussion but he'd be all right. Then they called again saying they thought he'd fractured his skull, but he was ok."

The next one said they were going to ambulance him to Idaho Falls, a larger town some ninety miles away, which had a modern hospital where he could receive specialized care.

And the last one said, "You'd better get down here right away, we're taking him into surgery."

It was terrible. As Mary Anne listened to each worsening message, her worry escalated from general anxiety over John's condition, to deep, desperate fear for his life. The perfect spring day had fallen horribly apart.

"I had to page my husband on the golf course, and it was dark before we were able to leave," she remembered. While waiting, she did the only thing she could do to help her son, crying out with every ounce of her mother's heart before God, asking Him to save her child.

"I prayed and prayed and prayed that God would send His angels to protect John," she said. "Not just one angel, but legions of them. I am a Catholic, and I prayed to Mary. I thought that if anybody knew a mother's suffering, she did, and she can intervene on our behalf with her Son. And He would surely listen to her."

All the way down from Helena, past the city of Butte and its copper mine, through the Big Hole Valley to Monida Pass, across the top of Idaho into the Snake River basin, through all those endless miles of mountains and valleys and hours of time, Mary Anne kept up her plea. *Please protect John and keep him well.* Watching the trees slide by in the night as they sped down the highway, her husband driving fast and silent as the stars hung high and white in the sky. One hour. Two hours. Three hours. Four. Her supplications rose to heaven on her mother's love.

"We didn't get to the hospital until after midnight," she said. "John was in intensive care, hooked up to all these machines, and the doctor had decided to delay surgery, so he hadn't had it, but he was unconscious—or sleeping." Which, Mary Anne wasn't sure.

"I am a speech therapist so I'm very familiar with head injuries," she explained. "The staff has like a test they do, called Orientation to Time and Place. They ask who you are, where you are, what you did today, who's the president of the United States. Sort of basic logical questions, to see if there's any changes in the brain.

"The nurses woke him up every half hour or hour to do this orientation, just to see how he was progressing. And the third time they woke him up, he couldn't answer the questions."

Unlike a lay person who would not have understood the significance of John being unable to answer these simple questions, Mary Anne knew exactly what was happening with her son. He was losing his tenuous hold on life.

"It was getting really scary," she said. "You could see the panic in the nurse, she started shouting at him, shouting the questions and he just kept saying, 'I don't know, just leave me alone.' And the nurse looked at me like, *He's really deteriorated, this may be it.*

"That same day, two other kids had hit trees on the same mountain and died. He was the third, and the nurse was indicating to me, 'This may be it now. Say goodbye.' And she said, 'I'm going to call the doctor.' And she left.

"I think it was about two or three in the morning by then.

"I just sat down on the chair by his bed, my heart was breaking, and I could see this mahogany coffin going down to his body. I put my head down, my head in my hands, and then I looked up, and the room was filled with angels. And it wasn't just one or two, it was like *legions* of angels. You could see row after row after row, as far as you could see. There were no walls in the room at all.

"And it just went on forever, this legion of angels, and then I heard a voice. Not a voice with my ears, but in my heart, saying, *John's going to be ok. I have other plans for him.*"

"The angels weren't vivid, I couldn't see details, like facial details, it was more like shadows. I could see the shadowy outlines of their wings, heads, and their bodies. It was like seeing them through a haze.

"Their wings were kind of straight, not open like the pictures you see of angels flying. You could see the hump where the wing goes and then they just dropped straight down at the sides. It just lasted a few seconds. I looked up and saw them, rows and rows and rows of them as far as I could see, and I heard the message, and I heard those words *clearly.*"

Just then the neurosurgeon came rushing into the room. She quickly stepped to the side of John's bed, looked him over and made a few changes. "Why did you call me?" she asked the nurse. "He's much better." Then she unhooked him from all the machines and moved him out of intensive care into the pediatric unit.

"That should have been a good sign for me," said Mary Anne, "but you know, I still doubted that he would be all right."

Mainly because every day, Mary Anne worked with patients who had suffered trauma to the brain. It was her occupation. She had seen brain injury many times, and knew its effects. Inability to speak. Unable to walk. Deciphering taken away. Understanding gone.

"Then I saw his MRI . . . or CAT scan, I'm not sure which one they had done, and I had just started working with a young man in Helena who had a head injury in an accident, and he had the exact same MRI as John had. He couldn't talk. He was paralyzed and in a wheel chair and had all these cognitive impairments. I thought, that's what I had to look forward to with John, because the MRI's were almost identical, in the same location of the brain.

"It was the left temporal lobe," she explained. "That is the language area of the brain. The brain is like a bowl of gelatin, and when the head gets hit on the one side, it slams the brain into the skull on the other side.

"So he had a huge bleed on that side of the brain, and another one kind of in the motor area. He shouldn't be able to talk today, and he should have had seizures. The doctor told me he would probably have them and he never did. It was frightening. I still can't look at those doctor reports.

"So, that was Good Friday," she recalled, "when they took John and put him in the pediatric unit. And by Easter Sunday they said, 'You know, he seems really fine. Let's send him home.'"

Mary Anne could hardly believe what the doctors were saying.

"This was going from Holy Thursday, thinking he was dying, to Easter Sunday—he's fine. Two neurologists and one medical doctor called it a miracle. And when they did the follow-up MRI here in Helena, there was nothing. Nothing on it."

Not a smattering of blood. No injury to the brain tissue. No broken bone. John's head did indeed seem to be perfectly well.

Even so, for the next three months, Mary Anne continued to worry about him. For in addition to the head injury, John had severed two arteries on the surface of his brain. If he was jostled or bumped or did jumping of any kind, an artery could rupture and flood his brain, killing him instantly.

As per the doctor's instructions, Mary Anne had his school teachers dismiss him early from classes so that he would not be bumped in the hallways walking to the next room. She forbid jumping, only to look out the back window to see him leaping up shooting hoops, joking with his friends, "This is the way I shoot when my mom's not looking."

"If I would have *believed* that I really saw those angels and heard that message from God, I wouldn't have had that terrible anxiety every morning," she told me. "Wondering, *Is this the last time I'm going to see John?* I come from a scientific background and am sort of cerebral. A part of me believed it, but then it was over and I wasn't sure."

But as she watched her son, as full of joy, life, and good health as he had been before going to Grand Targhee, when she thought again of those rows and rows of numberless angels, an army of God standing between him and death, as she played back the words only she had heard, the distinct message she knew came from God, something inside of her changed. What her mind questioned no longer mattered. Her spirit knew. And it was right.

"I *know now* it was angels," she stated.

"I believe He sent those angels to perform a miracle for John. And the biggest change for me is I have been able to give John back to God. I don't worry about him anymore.

I know that God's watching over him. He goes to Nepal where there's civil unrest and rebels in the street, terrorists all over with guns, and I just trust God."

Those words have become the theme of her life. And now hang above her door carved into a three-foot length of wood: "Trust in the Lord."

Reminding her every day of the miracle that is her son. John, healed. And that God does indeed hear our prayers, and sometimes, He sends angels to answer.

MICHAEL

It had been so long since I'd received an angel story, I was beginning to despair. How could I write God's book if I never heard from Him? Even while working it was on my mind, a continuous monologue running like water through everything I did. *When are you going to give me another story, Lord? How long do I have to wait, God?* Then the phone rang.

Beverly's cheerful voice flowed over the wires, my writing friend who understood the ebb and flow of inspiration and the solitude needed to put words on paper. A newspaper and magazine writer for many years, she had raised a large family on their wheat farm and still lived on the home place. Since we rarely got to visit, we kept in touch by email and phone calls.

"How is your book coming along?" she asked.

A sharp pain stabbed in my stomach. How could I admit that I was stopped, stock still, waiting on a story yet to come.

"You should talk to a fellow here in town," she went on, before I had a chance to reply. "His son saw an angel."

A lead weight dropped from my heart. Suddenly buoyant, I quickly fished a pen out of the drawer as she gave me his name, explaining that he taught at the school and had told about his son's experience in church one Sunday.

"I don't have his phone number," she said, "but you can ask the secretary at school. She'll tell him to call you."

Gratefully I hung up the phone, chastised and humbled yet again at the Master Plan of God and the list He has made in heaven. One that I couldn't see, order, or tick off, but which was numbered with every story I was to do, lined up, one after the other, with the time I was to receive them. The story of Michael was next.

The following day I called the school, wondering if they would be as trusting as Beverly thought. After the horrendous attacks on America by the rabid men of bin Laden, even we in Montana had pulled back, suspicious of strangers with an unknown name and face. The radical Muslims, filled with hatred, had shown us they were interested only in killing. It was their greatest joy. In that one second on September 11, 2001, as the planes floated through the metal and glass of the Twin Towers, slammed into the concrete of our nation's Pentagon, fell in a death dive to the soil of Pennsylvania, it became our responsibility to watch, be aware, and judge every man by his actions rather than his words.

So when the secretary at the school answered the phone, I carefully told her my name, gave her my address and explained that Beverly had suggested I contact them to talk to Michael's father. Instead of hanging up as I had feared, she courteously assured me she'd take my request and pass it on. He called back a short time later, curious and somewhat mystified, but as soon as I said that Beverly had heard him speak in church, he began telling about his son and the angel he'd met in the deserts of Arabia, a direct result of that terrible day when the sky filled with smoke and cries of anguish rose up from the souls caught in the clouds of death billowing around the crumbling Twin Towers.

Far away from his homeland of America, drawn into a war no human being should have to fight with oceans separating him from his family, Michael stared at the words on the computer screen in disbelief, trying to take away their finality, the message his father had emailed him from Montana in the middle of a cold February night. His grandmother was dead.

Sobs rose in his throat as he tried to think of how he could get back home, obtain authorization for a leave from his company, which had barely gotten set up after being deployed to the Arabian peninsula, where his fellow soldiers were fighting the Taliban after 9/11. Hardly considering the thousands of miles between Arabia and Montana and the fact that flights to and from his state could take days crossing Europe and the Atlantic Ocean, he only knew he had to get there to say good-bye to his grandmother.

I've got *to go to the funeral*, he thought. Hurrying to the phone, he called his dad and explained that he was going to contact the Red Cross for emergency leave. Within hours his efforts had failed, his request denied. He would not be allowed time to stand by his grandmother's grave as she was laid to her final rest.

Devastated, Michael called home again, the difference between the two worlds stark in his mind. On the Montana prairie, another winter blizzard raged, piling more snow in drifts across roads and fences already covered, stopping all traffic as plows became overwhelmed, unable to clear the highways due to the heavy snowfall and lashing winds. Relatives called in distress, stranded in motels and towns along the way as they tried in vain to drive to the funeral.

At his father's home, the phone rang constantly with messages of regrets and closed roads and the impossibility of going any farther, while at Michael's base in the desert, the heat, the sun, the sand felt like an unrelenting day in the hottest July. But on either side of the ocean, the grief was the same.

Grandma had been the pillar for Michael, "a tree planted by the living waters" as he grew up. Nothing was loved more than visiting her farm, the home which had sheltered his dad and her other twelve children, three of whom had passed away very young. The pioneer life on the prairie called her to years of labor, washing clothes on a washboard, churning butter by hand, baking bread in a wood cook stove, cooking huge meals for the threshing crews, all done with a serenity which caused her children to marvel. Never once did she complain. For deep in her heart resided the One who bears all burdens, heals all sorrows, gives strength in the midst of greatest fatigue. Nothing could separate Grandma from Jesus.

This love wrapped around all of her family, but none more than Michael, the first son of her youngest child. By the time of her death at 92, Michael had grown to a fine young man who had enlisted in the military, serving his country with the same diligence and determination she'd exhibited in all of her years on the farm.

Michael stared at the darkness outside his tent, trying to concentrate on work while his mind and heart were back home in Montana. When some of his buddies suggested a ride to town to eat supper, he decided to go along. Of the five friends who crowded into the land rover, only one, a Christian like Michael, knew that his grandmother had passed away.

Driving up to a restaurant that served American food, the boys hopped out and went in. As they were sitting around the table eating, an Arab man dressed in American-style clothing came up to the table.

"There was nothing out of the ordinary about him," remembered Michael. "He was dark haired with a mustache, fairly dark skinned, simply an Arab looking man. He seemed to be about six feet tall and of normal weight. His eyes were brownish although it was kind of dark in the restaurant so you couldn't really tell."

The stranger looked at Michael and began speaking to him in good English. Both of these things were unusual. None of the boys knew this man, most certainly not Michael, and many of the native people spoke only a smattering of English. Why had he approached them and singled out Michael? What was he saying to him? In confusion, the soldiers stopped eating, glancing at each other as the Arab man ignored them and continued talking.

He was sorry that his grandma had died, he said to Michael, but she wanted him to know that everything was okay.

"Your grandma is wearing a green locust necklace with a gold or copper chain," he said, "and she wants your mother to have it. Your grandma is fine and she and Wilbur [her husband] are together and he is showing her around."

As soon as the stranger started speaking, an odd warmth completely washed over Michael, heating up his face as the man spoke.

"I turned all red and it lasted until he was done talking."

What is going on here? he thought. *How does this guy know anything about that, all the way across on the other side of the world?* Confused, his friends stared at the Arab man. Was this some kind of a crazy lunatic? Should they prepare to defend Michael to keep him from harm? But the man ignored them as he continued to address Michael.

"Your grandma is excited that the whole family will be together for her funeral and that everything will be all right," the stranger continued. "She remembers all the time you spent with her and thanks you for it. Her favorite memory with you was when you were together in a sunflower field."

The only time Michael had been in a sunflower field was on a trip with his grandma to Minnesota for a family reunion. As they drove through the fields of North Dakota, they'd stopped to look at the sunflowers with their big golden heads drooping in the sun. Michael had never forgotten it.

With that, the stranger fell silent. As he stepped back, Michael struggled to force a word through his tight throat. "Thank you," he finally croaked.

"That was all I could get out," he said, tears breaking in his voice even then, three years after the strange visit.

The man turned away, walked to a table and sat down. Then, in full view of all six of the soldiers watching him, he rose from the chair, moved towards the exit and disappeared.

"He did not go and pay the cashier," said Michael. "He didn't go out the door, he just *left*. None of us could tell which direction he went or anything." As mysteriously as he had appeared, the messenger was gone. With a slight smile, his Christian friend caught his eye and shook his head in wordless communication. This was no ordinary visitor, he was saying. This man had come from heaven.

"What is going *on*?" burst out his friends. "What was that guy talking about?"

Dazedly, Michael told them that his grandmother had

just died, how he had loved her and tried so hard to get home to her funeral.

"My grandfather's name is an old fashioned Norwegian name," he said. "Hilmar, not Wilbur," he explained, his thoughts still whirling. How did that stranger know anything about his family? Who'd told him his grandmother had died? How could he describe the necklace she was wearing in the casket? Was she actually wearing one?

He went over the words the man had spoken again. Here he was, an Arab who'd walked up and told him all about his family back in Montana, information that was impossible for him to have. *Could he have been an angel?* The thought seemed fantastic and unbelievable, and yet logical, the only thing it could be. He had to call home and find out if Grandma was wearing a green necklace.

Hurriedly they finished eating and drove back to base with Michael desperate to get to a phone. Stabbing the numbers for overseas connection, he tried continuously for four hours before the call finally went through, zinging through the airwaves to outer space, down across the Atlantic and over the frozen miles of America, to jangle at the bedside of the darkened house, waking his parents in the middle of the storm swept night.

"Mom and Dad!" exclaimed Michael, panic sounding in his voice. "You won't believe what just happened!"

Barely able to speak through the tears coursing down his face, he told them how a stranger had come to their table at the restaurant and started talking about Grandma, assuring him she was ok and everything was going to be all right.

"He said she was wearing a green necklace in the coffin," he said, choking on his tears. "Is Grandma wearing a green necklace, Mom?"

The question tore his parents' self control apart. Choosing the piece of jewelry for his mother to wear had been the job of Michael's dad, and younger brother. Going to the nursing home, they walked down the hall to the room that had been Grandma's, the soft noises of the home following them as they pushed the door open and flicked on the light. Inside though, everything was different. Instead of a smile to greet them, there was only silence. Instead of warmth, a cool indifference. The inhospitality of an empty room.

Sorting through the beads filling her jewelry box, his dad noticed a jade green heart on a golden chain. *Where did this come from?* he wondered. Holding it up, he showed it to his son. "What about this one?"

"Yes," he nodded. Agreeing it would look nice on her, they pocketed the necklace and took it to the funeral home where it was carefully placed around Grandma's neck. Who knew? Other than those few members of her immediate family, no one. Most emphatically not a man in the far away deserts of Arabia.

But he had. An angel who had already spoken the words his mother would answer.

"Yes, Michael, she has a green heart necklace on."

LOIS

"Wanda, you've *got* to put an article in the paper."

I stood at the checkout desk of the library, laughing once more at our librarian's insistence while automatically preparing to say no . . . until I glanced up and saw the expression in her eyes.

Imploring. Beseeching. Asking please. Emmie Lou never asked for much. I'd known her since coming down to Circle years before, to work with my sister at the Traveler's Inn. While we cooked up the hamburgers and fries in the kitchen, Emmie Lou served them with sassiness out at the counter. Her infectious laugh and mischievous grin trotted right along with her to the library years later when she took over that job. One that had just lately come to include sorrow.

On a night when no one expected, without a hint of warning, our beloved volunteer, Betsy, heeded the beckoning finger of God and slipped away, hastening from this life to the next, while leaving a hole in our hearts that had not yet begun to heal.

"Betsy wanted you to," said Emmie Lou.

In an instant, I was back in Betsy's house, an uneasy

stranger in the crowd of women chattering in her living room. Having invited me to be the secretary for an organization I'd never heard of, *Christian Women's Club,* she'd met me at the door with a megawatt smile and enveloping hug. As if I were an old friend she'd missed so much.

What was it she exuded? Love? Yes, but more. Interest in others? Always. Enthusiasm? Effervescence would be more the word. She simply bubbled with joy. And carried everyone along with it. Months later, I asked why she'd selected me to sit on the board when she didn't know anything about me. For a moment she was silent. Then she spoke.

"Judy and I met with the others to put the board together. For each position we earnestly prayed for the right person, asking God to tell us who we were to ask."

Pausing, she went on, "Your name came to mind, over and over, so we figured you were the one we were supposed to have."

That obedience to God ended up feeding a hungry part of my soul as I attended the monthly meetings of the club, and gifted me with a friend I grew to treasure.

Ever since coming back from the *Guideposts* workshop in New York, where I'd learned how to write inspirational stories for the magazine, Betsy had urged me to put an article on it in our local newspaper. And now she was gone.

"Maybe you're right," I said to Emmie Lou. "Tell you what, let me think about it."

From the first time I picked *Guideposts* off the shelf in

the library, I'd loved the little magazine. Only about five by seven inches in size, with pages so thin I feared tearing them, every issue contained words straight from heaven. Simple answers to prayer. Astonishing miracles. Rescues by angels. Visits from Jesus the Christ.

I soaked them up, never failing to be humbled by the intricate workings of God. And when they published an invitation to submit an article for a writer's workshop, my heart leaped.

Every two years they set aside a week, flying the winners to Rye, New York, where they were schooled by the editors and writers of the magazine. People like Rick Hamlin, author of several books, Colleen Hughes, editor of *Angels on Earth,* John and Elizabeth Sherrill, writers of such best sellers as *The Hiding Place* and *The Cross and the Switchblade.* Immediately I sat down and wrote a story to send in. It did not win. Neither did the next. Or the next. For more years than I cared to remember I'd entered—and never been invited. So receiving a message saying I'd been chosen to go in 2004 seemed more a miracle than anything else.

The girls at the library were ecstatic. If possible, Betsy's smile glowed brighter and she beamed every time I came in. As soon as I got back, she started asking me to put an article in the paper. I always laughed and declined, explaining it seemed so like bragging, which I detested. That only made Betsy try harder. But she had never been able to convince me. And now Emmie Lou was asking for her.

What would it hurt, really? Maybe someone else *would* like to hear about my trip to New York. Even encourage them to write and enter the contest for themselves. After pondering all sides, I decided to honor Betsy's wishes and wrote an article. Calling the editor of the *Circle Banner,* I told him about winning the trip and what we learned at the workshop.

"Is there any other writing you're doing?" he asked, as we concluded the conversation. His query caught me off guard. The only thing was my book. God's actually. About His holy angels.

For a moment I debated. Would God want me to talk about that in the paper? How could I know? But would it do any harm? Quickly I tried to think of any possible problems. Finding none, I took a deep breath and explained that I was gathering stories about people who had seen angels, real angels, for a book I'd been working on.

The minute the paper came out, my phone rang with a call from our neighbor, Helen, who had been raised right up the road from my husband. As she told me about her sister being helped by an angel, I had to wonder if that was why Betsy had been so insistent in asking me to put an article in the paper on my trip to *Guideposts.* As close as she was to God, could it be that she had an inkling there would be a story for my book?

Just when Helen's sister Lois should have been doing nothing but enjoying her grandchildren, she found herself in the midst of the most trying time of her life. One of five children who grew up on a ranch in eastern Montana, Lois had always been terribly shy. The wife of an Assembly of God member, she and her husband had settled on a beautiful farm on the Flathead River outside of Kalispell, Montana. Peace flowed there like the waters burbling over the rocks. With the white-capped mountains around them and the evergreens lifting their fragrant boughs to the sky, each place she looked reminded her of God's majesty and glory. Until the sickness of her husband.

Cancer. Lois knew it well. An old adversary of their family, the insatiable disease had struck her mother, forcing doctors to amputate her right arm. For the rest of her life, her mom's sleeve hung limp, a constant reminder of what the killer could do. That loss never hindered her mother though. Instead, Elta's faith strengthened, shining like a light that could not be hidden. A constant smile graced her face. With sureness and determination she gripped the old black Bible in her remaining hand and encouraged everyone she met, telling them of the strength and ever abiding love of our Lord Jesus. It was as if the cancer had given her new life. A boldness to go where no one had gone before.

Such was not to be with Lois' husband. Rather than being stopped, the cancer spread from his colon to the liver. Hospital bills swamped them, especially since they could not afford health insurance. Worries, fear for her husband, and the insensitivity and outright badgering from those she owed money to, wore upon Lois day and night, culminating in a chance fall, when she tripped while walking across the yard at their farm, breaking a bone in her foot.

Unknown to her, the troubles besetting her would only worsen.

Nothing could be done to save her husband. On the day of his funeral, Lois answered the door to find the sheriff, boldly serving a summons demanding payment for their bills. The injustice, the total disregard for her grief and lack of decency to hurting people tore at her heart. Devastated by this callous indifference, she frantically searched for a way to pay the debts. Although urged to file for bankruptcy, Lois refused to.

"No," she stated, with a contrariness harkening back to her days of girlhood when she'd watched her parents wrestle a living from their ranch. "I'm going to pay my bills."

To do so would require another loss. The relinquishment of her farm. As the hounding from her creditors escalated, Lois was overwhelmed with another problem, keeping them from taking over her place. In desperation she cried out to the Lord, and He in His great mercy helped her, finding a way for her to sell the land which gave her the means to pay her bills, cut down on the hospital expenses and find a new home in which to live.

Surely this would be the end of her tribulations. It wasn't. They continued unchecked. In January, while going into the Perkins restaurant, she fell and broke both bones above the ankle in her right leg. With a full length cast from her hip to her toes, Lois was now unable to move. To walk or cook or do the simplest of chores about her house was impossible. Forced to enter a nursing home where she could be cared for properly, she spent her time lying upon a bed, waiting for her bones to heal.

Stationary and idle, a new danger emerged from her enforced immobility. Blood clots, forming throughout her injured leg. Any person, layman or medical, who has had experience with these tiny globules, knows how rapidly they can travel through the venous system to lodge in the lung, the brain, the heart, instantly causing a stroke, heart attack, or death. Fast and careful treatment prevented that from happening, and slowly Lois' bones knitted together until finally, they had healed.

In all that time, she had not been able to do anything at home, including the normal cleaning which every woman does. So, as soon as she was released from the nursing home, she tried to get started again on her housework, but her strength did not match her will, and too often, she had to stop before getting done.

One day, she decided to take a break and go to the local mall to get her hair done. As she left the beauty shop to return home, an older lady walked over to her and started asking about herself. Dressed in an old cotton dress just like

Lois remembered her Grandma wearing in the 1950s, there was nothing about the lady to make her look different from anyone else.

Except for one thing. She had the kindest eyes Lois had ever seen. Talking to the woman was so easy. Even when she presented Lois with an unusual request.

"Would you mind if I prayed with you?" she asked.

To Lois, it seemed the most natural thing in the world. Raised in a Christian family, married to a member of the church, prayer had been a part of her life since she could remember.

"I'd be delighted," she agreed. So right there in the middle of the shopping mall, the stranger stood and prayed for her.

Then she announced, "I am going to walk you to your car."

All the way past the shops lining each side of the mall, out the door and to the parking lot they went together, right up to the side of Lois' car, only two steps from the driver's door, where they stopped. Deeply grateful for the kindness and compassion the stranger had shown her, Lois moved up to her car door and turned to thank her. To her shock, no one was there! In the space of a breath, the woman had vanished, disappearing without a sound or movement, as if she had never existed.

Quickly Lois looked up and down the street, searching for the mysterious lady. Not one person was in sight. But that was impossible! How could anyone disappear in two steps?

Puzzled, wondering, disbelieving, Lois carefully got into her car and sat down. Who could it have been? Suddenly she felt infused with a vigor she hadn't felt in many months. Instead of driving home, she put the car in gear and drove straight to a car wash where she scrubbed her car clean. Going home, she commenced doing work a day before— nay, an hour before, she could not have done.

First, she took out the vacuum cleaner and went over all of her rugs, then gathered her cleaning supplies and swabbed down the shower in the bathroom. Still filled with energy, she unwrapped a new shower curtain that had been waiting to be hung and slid it onto the hooks.

All the while thanking God, for His providence, His guidance and most of all, for what she was now certain was, His angel at the mall.

ELOUISE

The most I knew of Elouise was her great kindness and welcoming spirit. A friend of my mother's from when they were young women, she and mom shared a love of good cooking, raising their children, and a subtle invisible bond I could never figure out. It was almost like they were sisters.

Although we seldom visited because of the distance between our homes, whenever I stepped into the cool darkness of her living room, I had only to look at her face to know I was safe. Somehow, an aura of goodness surrounded her. To my childish eyes she was tall, spare might be the word I would use today, though it was one I didn't know then. I could easily imagine her milking a cow or wielding a hoe in her garden, perhaps because I'd trotted along behind Mother as she did those chores, so it seemed natural that Elouise would be able to do them too. Yet, I'd never seen Elouise in anything other than a dress, usually a cotton print with a slightly swishing skirt, protected by an apron tied about her waist as she cooked and worked in the kitchen.

It had been years since I'd seen Elouise, so when Mother asked if I wanted to drive down to visit her in Glendive, I quickly accepted. All the memories came back to me when we stopped in front of the flat-roofed house, drapes tightly shut against the summer sun. She met us at the door as if she had been standing by the window, watching for our arrival, with the regal bearing I remembered so well. I sank into the comfort of her chair while Mom and she started talking, the murmuring of their greetings washing over me, as I leaned my head back in the quiet peace of her home and closed my eyes for just a minute.

I will have to ask Elouise if she's ever seen an angel.

Where did *that* come from! I shook my head and sat up in confusion, looking around for Mother. Had I inadvertently gone to sleep? Would Elouise think me so rude? Quickly I jumped up and followed their drift of voices to the dining room. Elouise's table spread out before them, laid with the best china and silverware, a veritable smorgasbord of meats, salads, pickles, fruit, and homemade bread covering every inch of the tablecloth.

"Elouise!" I exclaimed, shocked at the work she had gone to, preparing such an elaborate dinner for just Mother and me. "This is too much!"

She smiled and pulled out a chair. "No," she said softly, "it is nothing."

Today, after talking with her children, her son and two

daughters, I wonder if she knew it would be the last time she'd ever have the opportunity to seat Mother at her table. That the ticking of her days was racing toward its end and seeing Mother, sharing a meal with her, would never come again.

I sat down silenced, carefully taking a spoonful of each dish passed to me, determined to give Elouise the respect and honor she presented us. Then I asked to wash the dishes. She refused, insisting they were no trouble and calmly got up from the table.

While Mother went to the sink to wash her hands after eating, Elouise and I returned to the living room. As she settled on the couch, I took a chair at her side. *Am I supposed to ask if she has seen an angel, God?* I worried. *Do you really want me to?* No answer came. Did I actually expect one? But would there ever be another chance? I myself had grandchildren by then, and both Mother and Elouise had greatly aged. From sickness and death in my own family, I had learned how fast life can be over. Pushing down my hesitation to ask what she might regard as a personal question, I took courage in one hand and turned to her.

"Can you tell me, Elouise," I ventured. "Have you ever seen an angel?"

For a moment, I wondered if she'd heard me. She didn't move, lift a hand, or in any way acknowledge that I had spoken. Then she turned her head to the side, a faraway look coming over her face. I felt she was debating whether she should say anything. Then she said, "Yes. I *have* seen an angel."

"Oh, really!" I burst out, relieved I had not upset her. "Could you tell me about it?"

She began to speak, slowly, as if seeing again that time when she had been so young and God sent her answers in a way she never expected. "When I was a girl, my mother was going to have a baby and I wanted to know if it was a boy or a girl. I asked God to tell me what it would be."

She stopped and looked me full in the face, her eyes locked on mine. "One night I had a dream. In the dream an angel came. She was showing me it was going to be a girl."

"And was it?" I asked.

A little smile curved her lips, as if it was foolish and yet so typical for someone who hadn't seen it, to question a message from an angel.

"Yes. Yes," she said. "It was a girl."

I fell back, not even realizing until then how tense I'd been, waiting for her answer.

"How old were you, Elouise?"

"I was fifteen years old when that happened."

Old enough. To know the difference between an angel and a person in a dream. To recognize the angel's coming as being the answer to her prayer. To wait and see if it would be verified at the birth of the child. As it was.

Just then Mother came back into the room, ready to go

home, so I could only thank Elouise and prepare to leave. A short time later, she had to move to a nursing home because of her poor health. I made a special trip down to see her when I heard this, but it was too late. Unable to speak, lying with one arm in heaven, she passed away just days later.

It seemed such a short story. But Elouise was a devout Christian, and I was certain it was true. Still, I wanted to corroborate it if possible. Could she have told one of her children? Jim still farmed the home place. He might know.

"I have never heard anything, ever, mentioned about this, the story you are telling of Mother," he said when I called. "You know Scripture says that you may entertain angels unaware, and I have to leave it at that. There are people who obviously God sends in our way, to serve us in some capacity, did they come from heaven, or was it through His providential care that it was people, who were sent to bless us and help us here?"

How could I answer that? Only God knew. But Elouise had been sure. She knew it was not a human being, but an angel. But what did I know of her other than the impressions forged through childhood instinct. Maybe I should try to find out more about her family.

"How many brothers and sisters did your mother have?" I asked Jim.

"From her family?" His voice faltered over the phone. Warning signals clanged in my head. What was going on here? Why would Jim be hesitant to tell me about his mother's family? I waited, silence lengthening over the phone until he spoke again.

"Well . . ." he paused as if searching for the right words. "My mother was . . . she was born when her mom was sixteen."

Wow! I thought. *Awful young.* And then the truth of what he was skirting around hit me. Oh, no! Elouise's mother wasn't married! I cringed against this terrible reality. What a shame, what a sorrow for her mom and her parents. In the early nineteen hundreds, out of wedlock children were a great disgrace, with young women often thrown out of families. In thirty years of writing other people's stories, I had never run into this situation.

"She was raised thinking that her mom was her sister," Jim continued. "She was raised by her grandparents," he explained. "When she found out at age thirteen, it didn't go over well."

Dear God. My heart twisted for this young girl—two actually, both the mother and child. The elder forced to live with deceit in order to protect her family and stay in the community, the younger blindsided with a truth she could have never imagined.

"She got pretty rebellious," said Jim, "and ran off and got married when she was fifteen."

I reeled in my chair, hardly able to absorb all this when he added. "Well, we're talking hill folks from Kentucky here." And a great stabbing shock tore through me.

Kentucky! Elouise was from Kentucky!

Instant pictures of Grandpa's home at Mount Sterling, Kentucky flashed through my mind. The big white house. The two stately collie dogs guarding the front door. A wide yoke of oak wood, hand carved for a team of oxen, hanging on the dilapidated side of the old barn. A huge iron cauldron sitting by the step, offhandedly pointed to as coming from Boonesborough when Daniel Boone blazed through the Cumberland Gap. Rolling hills so tightly grown with trees and bushes I could not push a way through. Creeks, streams, water, everywhere, flowing through little valleys and down hills, spilling over rocks, pooling in still ponds.

Mother's home. Yes, she was raised in the sagebrush and gumbo of Garfield County in Montana, but her heart was in Kentucky. The place of Grandpa's birth. All of the reasons why Elouise and Mom got along so well clicked into place. They were of the same heritage. Children of the Kentucky hills. Sisters of the soul. Suddenly I understood why they melded together so well.

"She grew up in a place called Island, Kentucky," said Jim, "but she was actually born over in Talihina, Oklahoma. They moved to Montana in 1919, the first time she came up, and settled near Fort Benton. She was six when she was enrolled in school there, but they couldn't make it in Fort Benton so they moved back to Kentucky.

"I've got a picture of her standing on a plank, it's over a waterway so it must be the Ohio River. They were just subsistence farmers, had a little patch of tobacco, little patch of oats, raised a few geese and a couple hogs. That was what they did. They plowed with horses, fished the Ohio River, just kind of an agrarian, self-sufficient life style.

"The marriage didn't last long," he added. "When she was in her mid-twenties, she came back out here to Montana, south of Missoula at the Bitterroot to be with family, and that's when she met my dad. My aunt revealed some of this information to me inadvertently—-when I was 35, a very long time ago. She just couldn't talk about this stuff, cause to her, she would be betraying a confidence. To me, it wouldn't be, but people didn't open up and talk about things like that back then. I don't even know my mother's maiden name. Honestly. I *do not know* my mother's maiden name."

That would be his grandfather, I thought. All those years, through the humiliation and silence of the generations, Jim would never know who his grandfather was.

A sorrowing sadness filled me. How deep had this pain gone for Elouise? A woman to whom family was so important. Was it one reason why she loved children so much? Why she treated everyone kindly and with such courtesy? Because you never knew the story behind them? No one could bring back the phantom mother, the father that never was. But it was within her power to turn from that wounded past and become a loving, giving person. And that's what she'd done.

More surprises met me when I talked to her daughters. While Susan had never heard the angel story either, Elouise had told her of other happenings which occurred when her mother was expecting babies. Of six more children born to her mother, Elouise experienced a vision, before two were born. She was careful to use that term in speaking of it, never referring to it as a dream, and told Susan it was a vision of white doves flying around her bed, beautiful graceful birds, but winging silently, without making any noise. It made Elouise fear that something would be wrong with the child, and each time there was. Both of the babies were born deaf.

Nor was Elouise's other daughter, Sandra, familiar with the angel story, but she explained that Elouise was gifted with a sense of very strong premonitions and would know when things were going to happen. When I asked her if Elouise would have recognized the difference between the dream of the angel, and the visions of the doves, she adamantly said yes.

"She was raised in the Christian church, so far as I know she had always gone to Christian services as a kid, and was baptized at the age of 19 in the Green River in Kentucky, which was the way they did it in the South. She taught Sunday school and was a *wonderful* teacher. The gift of hospitality was truly her gift. When people came, they were always fed and taken care of. That was *very* much Mom.

"Yes," she said, "she would know the difference."

I came away from these revelations with more questions than when I started. What did the angel of the dream look like? Obviously it was a woman, for Elouise referred to it as a "she." Of course it had wings, because Elouise immediately recognized her as being an angel sent from God. Was she clothed in a beautiful white robe? Did she carry a little baby girl in her arms? Or did she have a sweet faced dolly that she held out for Elouise to hold?

None of these questions will ever be answered, and as I reflected on the hidden truth that had shaped Elouise's life, the strength and forgiveness she must have possessed to pardon what had surely been a wrong to her, but which at the time seemed to be the best decision for her mother and grandparents, the words Jim spoke came back to me.

"What's real is real, sometimes it's stranger than fiction." And who are we to judge?

GLORIA

A steady hum of voices buzzed around me as friends and neighbors streamed into the library, most of them stopping at the check-out desk to pick up a fresh baked cookie and glass of Christmas punch, while they waited to buy a copy of my book, *The Montana Cowboy*. Just published that fall, they beamed congratulations on me as they sat down in the old fashioned oak chairs and asked me to sign it.

A great swelling of gratitude filled my heart as I thanked them for coming, knowing so many had taken special care to attend the book signing that day. Some I'd expected, like our neighbor who had called earlier, asking me to save two books, others were a surprise, such as the widow of one of my high school classmates who had died the year before. Half of the afternoon had passed when I glanced up to see a friend from out of town. It had been ages since we'd run into each other and there she was, brown eyes dancing as she grinned at me.

"Gloria!" I laughed. "It's so good to see you!"

Gloria had raised a family while helping her husband in his work. Now a grandmother and widowed, she'd recovered from the grief of losing her husband and held a steady job herself. Piling her books and purse on the table, she immediately began apologizing for her wrinkled farm coat and blue jeans, explaining that she hadn't planned on coming to town that day, but there were some letters to be mailed . . . she needed to go to the grocery store . . . then she heard about my book and decided to stop.

I'd seen a lot worse clothes than hers, had *worn* them, and knew full well the heart of a person is of much more value than any of the feathers which might adorn them, so I waved away her explanations and started right in on visiting. Angels of course, were the last thing on my mind. But halfway through our catching up, a little nudge from nowhere, like someone poking you in the ribs, stopped me.

Ask her if she's seen an angel.

Ahhhh, I stuttered, trying to keep track of what Gloria was saying while attempting to analyze this silent but obviously clear suggestion. *I don't think Gloria has seen an angel!* I knew she went to church. Taught children's Sunday school. But thousands of people do that every week, and how many of them have seen angels?

Bringing my focus back to her, I started to hand her copy of *The Montana Cowboy* across the table when it happened again. This time more forceful and slightly demanding, as if the commandant would brook no refusal. *Ask her if she has seen an angel.*

I hesitated, studying Gloria's face, so full of fun and

life. Would asking her be an intrusion upon her privacy? Some people felt their beliefs and personal experiences were nobody else's business. Would she be upset or angry, or think it impertinent of me to inquire? But this prompting had not come from me, of that I was sure. And if God was telling me to ask her such an unusual question, He must have a reason for it.

Still I resisted, unsure, as Gloria picked up her book and set it with the ones she'd checked out from the library. She was getting her purse and starting to say good-bye. Suddenly I realized my time to ask was rapidly disappearing and if I was going to obey God, I'd better be doing it. Hurriedly I broke in.

"Gloria," I said, praying I didn't sound like a crazy person. "Have you ever seen an angel?"

The strangest look passed over her face. One which threw a barb of fear at me. Immediate wariness, followed by *why are you asking* and *are you sure you want to know?* In that instant, every noise and movement in the library seemed to stop, leaving us alone in a silent bubble, and though I remained seated in my chair, for a fleeting second it was as if I were standing in the far corner of the library, watching as a dome of clear shiny hard plastic settled over us, leaving us looking like little children sitting at a tiny table.

Just as quickly it was gone, and I watched Gloria deciding, seeing the expressions flit over her face as she weighed the information which only she knew. *Was it safe? Did she have the right? Would it bring harm? Could I be trusted?*

Suddenly she relaxed, a peace dropping over her body as she leaned back against the chair and nodded her head. "Yes," she said quietly, "yes, I have."

A shock of surprise electrified me. Hardly able to put a sentence together, I told her I was working on a book about people who had seen angels and wondered if she would be willing to tell me about it.

Indecision again brushed her features as she considered my explanation. Whatever had happened was serious and very important to her. As I watched her try to come to a decision, I determined to make no effort to sway her. The experiences of humans with God are often so holy, people want to shield them from others. And you cannot argue with that. I had done what God insisted. If Gloria wanted to tell me about it, she had the right to decide on her own.

A breath, a straightening of her spine, and she lifted her eyes to mine. Yes, she would tell me. But not there, in the library with people all around. Could I call her on the phone? Of course. So it was that on a quiet spring evening, I came to learn the story of Gloria's angels, and the reason why God had prodded me to ask that one simple question. *Have you ever seen an angel?*

It had not been an easy winter, for either Gloria or her daughter, who was getting a divorce. Every communication between the warring couple had been heated, with disagreements constantly flaring up. All through the process, Gloria's son-in-law had fought it through the court system, complaining about every little condition, again and again. And while he had promised to be decent to his wife during the proceedings, he wasn't. In whatever way he could, he worked to aggravate her, getting nastier and nastier, until the legal work which should have taken only two months had stretched far beyond.

The culmination came when Gloria and her daughter learned he had tried to find her at home alone one night. Knowing he was attempting to hurt her, her daughter finally had a restraining order put upon him. He had to keep away from her, the car, and the house. But even with that, Gloria worried. Having her own work and home to care for, she knew it was impossible for her to leave during the cold weather to protect her daughter so many miles away.

"I couldn't go down and live with her," Gloria said, "so I set out to pray that God would." Gloria had not always been that close to God.

"My dad was just about the biggest atheist you'd ever seen," she said. And after Gloria married and moved to the countryside, it was easier to stay home on Sundays than fuss with her husband about going to church. Even after losing him, it took too much effort to make it to town for services. After all, she wasn't going to die any time soon. She was healthy, happy in her work and certainly not that old. What could happen anyway? "I had to drive in to town one day to do some errands," she recalled, "so I put on my Eddy Bauer boots because I knew all of the sidewalks in town were covered with ice. Just as I stepped up to get on the sidewalk in front of the bank, my feet went out from under me and I came down *flat* and hit the back of my head on the cement.

"It gave me a severe brain concussion," she continued. "I couldn't stand light or noise, so I had to lie very still for days, to let things heal. And this may sound odd to you, but as I did that, I was thinking, 'I might not have lived through this.' And then I realized, 'There isn't a pastor in the area that could do my funeral. Nobody knows a thing about me.' Right then I knew I had to find a church home."

When she was able, she began going to church with her daughter who attended in town. "But I had my limits," she laughed. "I wasn't going to go every Sunday, and I told her I wouldn't teach Sunday school."

Some years before, Gloria had accepted Christ as her Savior at a different church. Eager to learn and grow in the Christian faith, she was stunned when neither the pastor nor the members of the congregation made any effort to welcome her or strengthen her fledgling faith. Afraid that might happen again, she hesitated to become involved with her daughter's church, but the minute she walked through the doors, she felt she had come home.

"When they started a new adult Sunday school class that was going to study the Bible from the very beginning, I said, 'That's what I need,' so I asked the pastor to come see me and he did." With his encouragement, she decided to take the class as well and dug out the Bible she had stashed at home, remembering exactly where she'd put it.

"Fourth drawer down in my dresser, underneath my red sweater."

It took a year for the class to go through the whole Old Testament. More to finish the New. All that time she continued attending church with her daughter.

"I was really riding on her coat tails," she said, "but one Sunday I went by myself. They started playing the invitation song, when the pastor asked anyone wanting to accept Jesus as their Savior to come to the altar, and it was my favorite song. "Just As I Am." I jumped to my feet intent on only one thing. Nothing would keep me from getting down there. A football player couldn't have done it better! I got up to the altar and went down on one knee, reaffirming the decision I had made for Jesus once before. Since then God has used me mightily, and He's equipped me all the way along."

Coming to God, learning about Him, talking with Him, eventually blossomed into a continuous conversation between Gloria and God, one which falls most easily under the heading of prayer. All those days and hours of speaking with Him brought Gloria so close to God that she felt easy discussing anything with Him.

"I have a very contented prayer life," she said. "It's just part of my life, not only in church, but at home, on the

road. Sometimes I wake up early and we, God and I, just
. . . commune, before I get up. Kinda like when somebody
asked Mother Theresa, 'What do you talk about with God?'
And she said, 'Well, I listen and He listens.' So for years, I
have felt very comfortable with God and praying."

But comfort fled when she found out her daughter's
husband was now threatening to harm her. Scared, worried sick that her daughter might be hurt, Gloria paced the
house, desperately asking God to do what she could not—
protect her daughter and keep her from harm.

Throughout the day, her petitions swept skyward.

"She's got to have some protection, God. Please, put a
protective barrier around her house. The garage. Her vehicles. The whole yard. Keep her safe on the way to work and
back home."

All through the night she sank before heaven's door,
imploring the Lord on behalf of her child. When the sun
broke, she arose with the prayer still on her lips, and in the
light of day, an unexpected sight came to her. The home of
her daughter, surrounded by angels.

"In my mind's eye," she related, "I saw a band of angels
around her house, around the whole property, and they
looked like," she hesitated, trying to find the right words. "I
would say, Zulu warriors."

"Zulu warriors!" I exclaimed. Those ferocious natives
of southern Africa who struck fear in the hearts of everyone
they attacked, including their own people. A flash of wild

whooping savages, brandishing spears and long shields burst upon my brain. Notorious for the fervor with which they fought, no force, even of contemporary soldiers, wanted to go up against the Zulu warrior. And these were what God had put around the home of Gloria's daughter?

But what did these angels look like? Did they wear the native dress of the tribe? Feathers, animal skins, bright beads woven in intricate designs? Wait a minute. The Zulus were Africans. Were the angels as well?

"Were they black?" I asked Gloria.

"No," she replied, "but they were tall, fierce, they were very fierce, there was nothing fluffy about them. And they were just side by side by side by side, ringing the perimeter of what she owns."

"Can you tell me how they were dressed?" I asked her.

"Well," she paused to think a minute. "Not as a head dress type, like an American Indian warrior. More of what I think of tribesmen somewhere, in any part of Africa. It was just as if you took up a bunch of Zulu warriors, that's what they struck me as. There was clothing on them, but I don't know what it was. It wasn't pants, and a rifle or anything like that. It was much more of the tribal warrior. I can't say that I saw spears, but they were . . . *powerful* looking."

"The odd thing was," she added. "They were facing IN, looking *at* her house. It was like I was standing in the neighbor's yard, looking at them, and they were ringed around her property line, side by side, all the way around it, facing

IN, protecting. I was thinking later, why weren't they facing OUT? But, that's the way I saw them."

I tried to imagine the angels stationed around her daughter's home. Were there five, ten, on each side of the house?

"How many were there?" I asked.

"Oh," she responded. "If you would take a half acre lot, and they stood side by side all the way around it, I don't know. A couple hundred?"

"Two hundred!" I gasped.

"It would have to be," she said. "If a lot is a hundred feet long, and they're two feet per person, that would be fifty, fifty, fifty, fifty. They were close. Right side by side."

A small army. An impenetrable barrier. It was clear to me God was making sure no danger of any kind could get to Gloria's daughter.

"Do you remember if they had wings?" I asked.

"No, they did not," she said firmly.

Hmmm. So the Zulu warriors did not need wings to do their work here on earth.

"What did you think this was?" I asked her. "Would you call it a vision?"

"Oh, yes," she replied. "It happened during the day, not while I was sleeping, and I got the sense of 'Oh! That's what I'm being shown. That's what's happening down there today.' It was like an answer from God, telling me. 'I'm going to show you what I have around her place. Then you can just put it out of your mind. She is protected.'

"It was just this *click*. And I saw them for a few seconds. And *click,* it was gone, and God saying, 'This is what I'm doing down there. It's done.' And that was IT!

"I knew she was being taken care of, and I did not have to worry anymore," she said, sounding relieved. "And she had no more trouble from her husband at all."

For a moment Gloria was quiet, thinking back on that image of the wingless warriors taking care of her daughter, and the great compassion of God to not only answer her prayers, but to give her the reassurance she needed by dropping the scales from her eyes so they could be seen. A sight she will never forget, and one which illuminated a side of God she had not previously considered.

"It showed me He is not passive," she said. "He's very active. Sitting. And sharp with a two-edged sword."

Ready to do battle, around a young woman's house.

JEAN

The big double doors of the old Quonset yawned wide as I passed through, barely avoiding a flurry of grade school kids, laughing and talking in their bright polished boots and brand new blue jeans. 4-H members, getting ready to show their animals at the county fair.

High above, the heavy steel walls curved in a half circle over my head, reverberating with the noise of happy chatter as I moseyed down the aisles between the shelves of exhibits, looking at the entries that had come in for judging the day before. Satin blue ribbons draped over jars of chokecherry jelly and fat dill pickles. They flowed down the fronts of home sewn cotton shirts and Pendleton wool suits, and were laid upon rich brown wallets and hand-tooled western belts where the leatherworking rested.

Occasionally, a bright multicolored rosette proclaiming "Best of Class" was prominently displayed upon an individual work. Getting that award at the fair was a big honor. Even in our small town, the competition ran deep, from Grand Champion Steer to best crocheted doily. The work. The pride. The time and effort to make it right, all spoke through the perfectionism of each individual piece.

Stopping beside the fresh flowers to admire what the other women of my community could do and I couldn't—raise beautiful flowers—I glanced up to see one of my friends weaving her way around the tables. Jeanie, who occasionally entered her lovely flowers in the fair, and generously spaded up plantings from her garden for me to try. Ones which invariably, never survived. Still, we kept trying, and I always cheered for her entries to win.

I turned with a smile, eager to learn what she'd brought in this year, before noticing a tall, stately woman walking beside her. One who seemed vaguely familiar, although I was sure we'd never met. Something about the way she moved, the expression on her face tugged at my memory.

"Wanda," said Jeanie, introducing us, "this is my classmate, Jean Sorley."

Sorley? I dredged back in my mind for where I'd heard that name before. Ah . . . yes. Peggy Sorley, a joy-filled Christian if ever I saw one. Peggy and her husband farmed for many years up by Vida, and she had been a part of our Christian Women's Club when we met in Circle. Jean's face held the same look of unhurried peace I remembered from Peggy's. What was it anyway? Tranquility? A deep core of calmness, as if nothing could shake her? That was the resemblance. Jean looked just like her mother.

We formed a little island in the middle of the fairgoers, talking about the exhibits and Jean's visit back home. At a pause, she stopped and asked. "What do *you* do, Wanda?"

"Well," I said, "we farm west of town, up Horse Creek."

"Wanda also writes," added Jeanie, smiling at me. "She's a writer for *Guideposts* magazine."

A spark of interest lit Jean's eyes, which oddly caused me to think immediately of my angel book, the project I rarely talked about, especially to strangers. But Peggy's big smile flashed before me and suddenly I knew she would have loved it. And Jean was so like her mother, wouldn't she as well?

"I'm also working on a book about people who have seen angels," I ventured. "Have you by any chance ever seen one?"

A sort of stillness caught her. Almost as if her spirit, the life of her soul, had suddenly been swept away, leaving the shell of her body empty, rigid, unable to move. The reaction startled me. Had I caused her to recall a painful memory? Crossed a boundary I didn't know existed? Was there something about angels that upset her?

Slowly she let out a breath, and the naturalness came back with a slight shake of her head. "Why, yes," she said quietly, still seeming to be miles away from this fair grounds, these busy people all around us. "I believe I have."

Relief flooded over me. She understood. And there in the midst of the fresh baked bread and sweet apple pies, she agreed to tell me about it.

Jean had grown up on a farm almost halfway between Circle and Wolf Point near the little community called

Vida, my backyard really, for our family had lived in Circle after Mother and Daddy married, and we had moved to our farm southeast of Wolf Point after his heart attack.

"We went to a one-room schoolhouse," Jean recalled, "just south of Vida. It was out on the prairie, not far from where we lived. I don't know what happened to the building, there's just an empty field now, but I did find the old pump and got a picture of it."

Schoolhouses dotted the prairie back then. Every township had two sections of land which were set aside as trusts to be used for income to maintain country schools. Built solid and square, always painted white, the school's large open room housed students from grades one through eight. Outside, often close by the front step, a well for fresh water was dug, which had an iron pump jack sticking up above the casing. With a few quick strokes of the jack handle, cold, clear water came gushing out of the spout, splashing into the students' cupped hands as they caught a drink, or sloshed water over their faces to cool off after playing outside the school at recess. When Jean said she'd gone to the country school, it surprised me for I'd thought she had always attended the Vida school, where her mother had taught for years.

While most of the land around Vida has now been plowed up into fields, when Jean was growing up, much of it was still native grass. "My most favorite times were saddling my horse, then riding the many miles of pasture," she remembered. "Taking in the fresh air, cool breeze, and the stillness of being the only ones to enjoy that moment." Just Jean and her horse. A feeling I knew well.

A rapport seemed to stretch between us. My father's farm had been about twenty miles north of her family's place, and the one thing I loved to do, too, was swing on a horse and go for a ride. As she told me about it, a little corner of my heart wished we could have lived closer to each other and gone riding together.

The wonderful faith of Jean's mother and father grew in Jean's heart like the well-watered grass of her beloved prairie. From them she soaked up the tenets of Jesus. *Thou shalt love the Lord thy God with all thy heart, and all thy soul, and with all thy mind. This is the first and great commandment. And the second is like unto it, Thou shalt love thy neighbour as thyself.*

Every day, whether it was her mother in the classroom with her students, her father inviting friends to boat on Fort Peck Lake, or just visiting with neighbors, her parents brought those words to life. Kindness, generosity, caring, thoughtfulness, compassion, giving, welcoming. Spreading joy. Helping others. And of course, praying. The silver thread ran through all of their lives, and Jean came to realize that one of her greatest joys was praying for people who were ill.

One day Jean's daughter invited her to a church service which would include a visit by a gifted healer. Jean immediately accepted, for it gave her the opportunity to once again help those who were sick by praying for them. At the meeting, the doctor, a practicing chiropractor before becoming a spiritual healer, invited any person who needed healing to come forward, tell him of their problems, the pain they were having, and then lie down on a table placed before him so that he could pray for them.

When one responded to the healer's invitation, the rest of the congregation was asked to close their eyes and concentrate on the healing for him as the doctor began to pray. Immediately Jean did so, adding her silent prayers to the ones the doctor spoke out loud as he asked God to heal the illness.

A deep quiet fell upon the sanctuary as the prayers of the petitioners rose. But Jean struggled to keep her eyes closed. An energetic person who liked to know what was going on, she found it difficult to keep from watching the healer. Maybe it was her intense curiosity. Perhaps she just wanted to see a holy man at work. Whatever it was, it wouldn't take long. *I just want to peek,* she promised. *Just for a brief second.* As her eyelids fluttered open, she glanced up and froze.

For stationed high above the doctor, high . . . high above him, stood a living, breathing woman. With her head bowed and hands held together in prayer close to her chest, she appeared to be praying along with the healer.

Oh, my gosh! gasped Jean. *What am I looking at?*

"She was the most beautiful woman I have ever seen," Jean said, a note of wonder still in her voice. Incredibly tall, the woman stood motionless within a softly glowing cloud of white, with both the details of her head and the robe she was wearing shaded in various hues of soft blue colors.

"The image was so clear, I thought for sure she had to be a living being," recounted Jean. "She was alive there in front of me, so elegant and soft looking. And in the next instant, my brain sort of started engaging and I thought, *Oh, I'm not seeing right.* I blinked a couple of times, closed my eyes and thought, *Ok, it's just the light. It's just something.* But she was definitely a *woman*. And it was sooooo clear, I thought I could just walk up, go to the front of the church and touch her. It was incredible.

"As I held my gaze upon her, for what felt like a long time, my eyes automatically blinked and her image was gone." Leaving Jean with a feeling of deep comfort, a kind of serene, no worries, surreal type of joy and well-being which reminded her of the times riding horseback alone, across the wavy grassland of Montana.

To this day, Jean's thoughts hold on to this experience, the astonishing appearance of an unexpected angel, guarding the moment while at the same time hoping to see her again. "It was almost as if I wasn't really present in my body," she marveled. "Like I was floating, just *seeing* this image. But it is so real, every time I think of it I could be there today, and I still see her."

Why did God give this girl of the prairies a vision of His angel while keeping it hidden from all the others? Was it because she opened her eyes in the midst of the prayers? Did God know her heart, how compassionate she was and the depth of her desire to help others? Or did He just decide to give her what she'd wanted, a little peek, only for Him it was a much larger one, a little peek of heaven, by letting her see the helper He'd sent down to pray, the beautiful angel from heaven.

CHERIE

The eyes of Cherie flashed like lightning as she strode into the little café and pulled out the chair opposite me. They skewered me with a pulsating energy that seemed to leap out of her spirit. As I sat riveted behind the table, I suddenly realized those startling eyes were colored gray. A beautiful deep, clear gray unlike any eyes I had ever seen.

I've looked into indigo blue, sky blue, chocolate brown, autumn hazel, sea green, and Indian black, but never in my life had I gazed into eyes such as those. A true slate gray full of fire and life, without one speck of off color marring their smooth iris. For the first time in my life I understood what Jesus was talking about when he said the light of the body is the eye. Cherie's entire being vibrated with it, blazing out through the doorway of her soul, and though I'd never met her before, at that moment, I knew this Cherie was not your average person.

I'd been introduced to her through essential oils, the same frankincense and myrrh given to Baby Jesus by the wise men, when I was looking for something to help my headaches. Somehow, as we visited over the phone, our talk turned to angels and when I told her I was writing a book

133

on them, she immediately offered to tell me how angels had been her playmates and companions since she was a child. As we settled down behind tea and a glass of cold water in the café, the story she told of her angels showed me how remarkable her life had been, and continues to be today.

"It happened a couple of days before Christmas in 1990," she began. "A few days before, I'd found a large, black lump under my tongue on the right side of my mouth. It was about the size of a shooter marble. I went to the doctor and he lanced it to do a biopsy."

Hesitantly, as if she still didn't want to acknowledge it all these years later, she added, "A lot of . . . *stuff* . . . came out."

Her voice dropped, as she relived being in that examination room, leaning back, mouth stretched open, daring not to move as the doctor carefully inserted the knife and cut into the strange lump. Which immediately gushed forth a vile stream of infection and pus.

"There was a lot," she explained, and I could almost see her shudder, feeling helpless as the nurses thrust clean white gauze and fresh cotton into her mouth to catch the unexpected flow, to keep it from spilling out upon her face.

"It was black," said Cherie, looking at me with those marvelous eyes, and I almost threw up. Black was death. Discharge that color could mean only one thing. Cancer.

She paused, saying those words again, hard. More to herself than to me.

"It was *black, black, black.*"

As if wishing she could have spit that lump out, and with it, the poison that threatened her life. I have never worked in a doctor's office, but I could imagine her horror at seeing this black gunk spewing out of her mouth, and knowing that she'd have to wait days to find out what it meant.

"On Friday night," she continued, "about 8:30 pm, I got a phone call. It was the doctor himself. I'd just gone to the clinic and they picked out a doctor from their staff who I'd never met before, so I was really surprised when he called me at home, so late at night.

"'What are you doing working on a Friday night?' I asked.

"'I'm going to take a two-week vacation with my family,' he explained, 'and I need to talk to you. Is there anyone there with you?'

"I was in the lower level of my house wrapping presents for my family for Christmas and had music on the stereo. I was very joyful because I love Christmas, but I was alone, so I said, 'No, there is no one else here.'

"He goes, 'Well, you have . . .' and he said a string of words I wasn't familiar with.

"'What's that?' I asked.

"'Cherie,' he said, 'it's cancer.'

"It didn't even faze me. I just said, 'Ok, we'll take care of it.' And hung up the phone."

I caught my breath in astonishment. Didn't this girl know the seriousness of what the doctor was saying? Did she not realize the battle ahead of her, the surgeries, chemo, radiation, the possible loss of some of her tongue, her jaw, the inability to swallow, to speak? How could she be so cavalier about it, so offhand? Before I could pull out any one of those questions, she went on.

"Two minutes later, he called me back. 'Is there anyone else there with you?' he asked again.

"'No,' I said, 'it's ok.'

"He must have realized he couldn't do anything else, so he said, 'I'll be gone two weeks, and when I get back, I'll talk to you.'

"'Ok,' I told him. 'Have a wonderful vacation.'"

Her pragmatic attitude rattled me. How could she be so unafraid, act like it was not important? *Cancer? Oh, yeah, we'll take care of that.* Like it was a simple cut to bind up or a scratch on the knee. And who was this *we* anyway? I'd known quite a few people who'd had cancer, and doctors, nurses, radiologists, therapists, husbands, wives, mothers, and daughters often couldn't do a thing, but watch. The soft tone of Cherie's voice interrupted my thoughts as she continued telling me what had happened that night.

"I hung up the phone and turned around," she said, her voice slowing down, a touch of awe slipping into it, "and the room was *glowing*. It was so bright and light. I felt . . . and *saw*, all these angels."

Scooting her chair back from the table, she stood up and held her hands horizontal, palms facing each other about eight inches apart, and then spread them higher. "They were individual lights, of all different sizes. I would say they were from eight to nine inches tall, to very, very large, just below the ceiling. They were everywhere. Everywhere!" she exclaimed, a huge grin splitting her face.

Switching her hands around, she opened them across her body, showing a thin two inches. "Some were skinny," she said. "And some were wider." Pulling her hands a good foot apart.

"The color differentiation was very subtle. They were versions of a bright, kind of golden, white light.

"It was gold, yellow, white, really white, like glistening snow. Bright, but it didn't hurt your eyes. They were not like the angels people paint, with wings and all. I could not see any bodies, any clothing at all. They were energy spirits. The room was filled with it. *Filled!*

Sliding back into her chair, those mesmerizing eyes flashed at me. "There was a bunch of them. Two dozen? Twenty to twenty four? I'm not sure. We had a crowd, and the angels were having a party."

She started laughing. "It was happy," she said. "The room was full of joy. I felt so safe, secure, like everything was going to be ok. I had Christmas carols on the cassette tape and the biggest smile inside of me. I *love* Christmas music, but there was no music or sound with the angels. They came to heal me, but what do you think? They came to play with me! We were having a Christmas wrapping party." And I could just see that Cherie cutting up paper and snipping off ribbons, singing along with the music while the angels danced around her.

"The room stayed aglow pretty much the whole night," she said. "I just looked around, watching them all. I wasn't scared at all. They stayed until I was done. Then it was like, OK, presents are wrapped, time to go to bed. And that was it. They were gone."

Cherie sat for a moment quietly, her eyes cast down. "I went to my holistic doctor the next Monday or Tuesday and told him what the diagnosis was," she said.

"'How'd you like to take care of this?' he asked me.

"'Well,' I said, 'I feel like I'm already heading in that direction. I'm supposed to go back in two weeks, how about we have it handled by then?'

"'Sounds good to me,' he said, and that's where we left it.

"I had my stuff to do for Christmas and I totally forgot about it. When I went back to the medical doctor the two weeks later, he looked for it and it was gone." Her eyes sparkled with a mischievous twinkle.

"He was shocked. All he could say was, 'It's unexplainable! An unexplainable occurrence,' while he probed around in my mouth. I didn't tell him it was my angels," she laughed.

That was because Cherie had a long experience of telling people about angels, and most of it was bad.

"I was raised Old World Lutheran. There were five of us kids, in Minnesota. We were German, and were not allowed to talk; only if my father talked to us could we talk. He was in the military, a strict disciplinarian, so he was gone a lot.

"I first saw angels when I was very little. I remember laying in the crib seeing them, watching them dance around me, when I was maybe two or three years old. I thought that was the way it was with everyone. For me it was normal.

"As I grew older I would talk to them, and they would answer me. They all had faces, some had bodies, and they were all soft and kind. I didn't realize no one else could see them. That was a gradual process for me, and it was very hard. Because I would tell my sisters and they would go in and say to my mom, 'Mom! Cherie's lying again! She's telling stories again!' And my mom would take the bar of Lava soap and wash out my mouth. Even as a tiny little girl. So I learned to not say anything."

The injustice of this terrible treatment, to a very small child who was only saying what she knew to be true, set my teeth on edge. Lava soap is horrible. A sickly green, it contains pumice and more ingredients to cut through heavy grease, and was made for men who worked as mechanics and laborers. Many times I watched my father turn on the faucet and run that thick bar of soap under the water, trying to work up a decent lather to get the oil and grime off of his hands. I couldn't believe a mother would actually take it and scrub the suds into her little girl's mouth with a washcloth. No wonder Cherie stopped talking.

"Then in 1986 when I was a young woman," she continued, "I had a car wreck. I was watching my body from above it. I had really bad brain and spinal cord injuries. A spirit came and got me. I knew we were going to heaven. He was dressed in a long dark robe of soft grayish colors. I wasn't afraid, but I didn't want to go, and I paused.

"'Do I have to go?' I asked him. He stopped. 'No you don't,' he said.

"'Then I don't want to go,' I told him.

"Three times he asked me. To make sure. Because I was really hurt. And then I went back.

"I lost my sense of who I am. I couldn't hear or feel God. I couldn't hear or feel the angels. I lost *everything*. All I could feel was the intense pain of the injury. It was one of the worst times in my life.

"But I gained compassion through that, because I learned from a wonderful counselor that this was what the average person's life was like. What was normal to me—having angels around at all hours of the day or night, was not normal for everyone else. And I'm like, *How can they function?* So I have a lot more compassion and understanding now for people. If there's one gift that came out of all that, that was it."

Great pain and hurting showed in her eyes as she stopped and looked at me.

"There have been so many unexplainable things happen in my life," she said softly. "Of angels or God. It cannot be anything else. They are there all the time. You can't see them. You have to believe. Because they are on a different dimension, frequency, it's beyond faith, beyond belief.

"Number 1 is Hope.

"Number 2 is Faith.

"Number 3 is Believe.

"Number 4 is Knowing."

A big smile lit her face. "You get to "knowing" and you can see them and feel them all the time. They are there. We were created to help and support each other. When we need help, all we have to do is reach up."

I pondered those words long after Cherie waved her good-byes.

Hope . . . Faith . . . Believe . . . Knowing

Where was I in that school of learning? Did I have hope in God and the angels of heaven? Absolutely. Many times He had come to the aid of my family and loved ones, sent angels to help. This I knew. Had seen in others. How could I strike that most precious hope from my heart?

Faith? Just because I had never seen an angel, was I to declare they do not exist? Or was I to take the word of the Most High and combine it with the truth I knew to be from people on earth who had been given that sight? As Paul the servant of God told us in Hebrews 11:1: *Faith is the substance of things hoped for, the evidence of things not seen.* Oh, yes. We have the evidence of invisible angels, their form and shape made visible to ones who pleaded for God to send them, as well as ones who unexpectedly were given the ability without heavenly petitions. With that solid proof, how can I not have faith that angels rush to our side at the first word from God?

And so I believe. Totally. Completely. Without reservation. It is not a question. To others I leave the debate, the endless probing and denials, the forever "show me" and "unless I see it with my own eyes." Another man spoke those words some time ago and lived to be chastised for his disbelief. I would rather not be thus reproached by one much higher than I.

But knowing. That stops me. Are there really angels around us all the time as Cherie insists? Does God care so much that He will never leave us alone, even when it seems that we are? Does He only ask these four simple things for us to be aware that they are but a breath away?

If so, I must work on my knowing, and thank God for sending me the teacher with flashing eyes so that I might learn some of these mysteries of God.

KARI

He did not believe in angels. Actually, he didn't believe in God. An atheist, a medical expert, a hands-on . . . show me the facts . . . if I can't see it, I won't believe it . . . kind of man, who took that way of thinking into his office—the hospital.

I never knew him. It was only through visiting with another woman that I came to know of his existence. He was her doctor. The day she died.

Kari's unique mouse repellent had intrigued me since the first time I saw an ad for it in a local newspaper. Made of all natural materials with no poisonous chemicals, it was guaranteed to keep mice and rodents out of tractor cabs, combines, trucks and other farm vehicles which are commonly parked for months at a time during the winter. Since mice in our equipment was a constant problem, I started looking around for this unusual Fresh Cab repellent, and put it in our outfits as soon as I found it. It worked, which caused me to wonder about the young woman who had invented it.

When I learned she was a farm gal who lived just across the border in North Dakota, I asked the editors at

Guideposts magazine if they would let me write an article on her struggle to perfect the repellent. They agreed and a short time later I was calling on the phone, never dreaming she would tell me how creating the mice deterrent had put her on a path which would imperil her life and cause God to place an angel between her and heaven's door.

Kari loved living on the farm amongst the acres of wheat and corn which grew in the rich black earth north of the Missouri River in North Dakota. A former city girl, her spirit bloomed in the country like the flowers she tended, as she worked in the gardens she planted around her home for both beauty and nourishment. Flower petals, mixed with aromatic oils and ground up corn cobs, were made into fragrant potpourris which she sold to local businesses for gifts. Vegetables raised organically she took to the farmer's market for people who wanted to eat foods grown without sprays and chemical fertilizers. And in her spare time, she experimented with trying to figure out how to develop a mouse repellent. One that didn't kill the animals with poisons, but sent them skedaddling away as soon as they smelled it. For years, she'd tinkered with it, considering it her hobby, never getting it quite right, always trying something new, until one hot summer day in July, 1995.

That morning, Kari gathered up the fresh produce from her kitchen garden, the early peas and lettuce, spinach and greens, which had just started to come on, put them into her car along with a table and chair and headed for the farmer's market in Stanley. In a short time she had set up her display, and was chatting with the girl at the next table who had brought two large trays of hydroponic tomatoes to sell. Because of it being early in the season, traffic was slow at the market with only a few pedestrians wandering around the tables.

Each week the town of Stanley sectioned off the area around the farmer's market so shoppers had a quiet place to browse and walk without worrying about being in the way of cars driving on the street. That morning however, the roadblocks did no good, as a woman, out of control on a huge motorcycle, roared past them and into the selling area where the booths were located.

"If you could picture this," Kari explained. "A seventy-two-year-old lady. On a touring bike. A Gold Wing Honda. With a side car. She came into the farmer's market at about eleven in the morning, wearing leathers, high heels, and her long gray hair pulled back in a ponytail. Somehow she panicked. She lost control, and her bike ran into the table of the gal next to me who was selling the tomatoes.

"I was between the two tables, and the force sliced my leg off. In half. At my femur. I didn't realize that. I thought my knee was broken. It knocked me out and I ended up laying on the pavement on a bunch of the smashed up tomatoes.

"When I came to, people were crying out, 'Oh, my God!' and I was trying to calm them. It was extremely painful, but I said, 'Naaaw, it's just a broken knee' because I didn't know what had actually happened.

"The lady who ran the market came rushing up, her face so blue I thought she was dying.

"'Kari!' she exclaimed. She didn't know what to say or who to call for help. Suddenly, a phone number popped into her head. She knew instantly it was from God and called it, having no idea who it went to, and it was the emergency department.

"The EMTs came, and they didn't hardly know how to handle it. They picked me up to put me in the ambulance, and the last thing I said was, 'Oh, no! How am I going to take care of my garden?'"

But at that moment, Kari was the only one worried about her garden. The EMTs had a much more desperate job on their hands. Keeping her alive. With her leg cut in two; bone, muscle, nerves and veins crushed and severed, they worked frantically to stabilize her as the ambulance raced down the endless road to the hospital, fifty long miles away. Fighting to maintain her vital signs while keeping her stable to prevent the femoral artery from its eminent rupture, they sped to the Minot Trauma Center, knowing her condition was far too critical for admittance to the smaller hospital in Stanley.

Screaming up to the emergency room with lights flashing and sirens wailing, the EMTs wheeled her out of the ambulance and into the hospital. Without wasting a second, nurses rushed her to the operating room, where a surgical team had filled the OR, waiting for her arrival, because every doctor and nurse, including the head surgeon, knew her life was hanging by a thread, for once the femoral artery bursts, a person has just minutes to live. As he rapidly assessed the traumatic injury, he realized that in order to save Kari's life, they might have to amputate the mangled leg. How do you tell a vibrant, young woman, with a husband and two small children, there is a good chance she will lose her right leg and be crippled for the rest of her life? He did it the only way he knew how. Quickly. Truthfully.

The possibility vibrated through Kari's subconscious. She never imagined losing her leg; a break she could handle, even though it would take time to heal and mend. A broken knee could be saved, but losing her leg entirely? As she sank toward unconsciousness, the question neither she nor the doctor could answer flickered through her mind.

When I wake up, will I have one or two legs?

"I was coming and going, in and out of consciousness," Kari remembered. "Everybody was scurrying around, blood was flying everywhere. It was a crisis moment."

One that was so critical, even in her dying condition, Kari felt it. Which way would she veer as they fought to save her? Towards life? Towards death?

In the desperate room, seconds ticked by, each one a prayer that Kari might be given more days, hours, years yet to live. That there was a whisper of a future, solid and secure, waiting beyond the hospital walls. Then her heartbeat faltered. The lungs fell, empty and lax. And her next breath stopped. Still and silent on the operating table beneath the hands that had sought to save her, Kari lost the battle for her life.

The head surgeon paused, instantly alert to the change in his patient. Eyes flashed to the clock. And widened in disbelief as they lifted to see a sight he had argued could never be. A gloriously beautiful angel, as clear and distinct as every other person in the room, hovering directly above the body now lying limp upon his table. Enveloped in a glow of shimmering white light, the angel stood over Kari unmoving, as if it had come on one mission only. To protect her body. To bring it life.

All those old beliefs, those *certainties* of the head surgeon, fell away before the presence of this magnificent winged being. How could he refute an angel of God, standing right above him? It lived! Where did it come from? No place on earth, that he was sure. No man, no one in the operating room could have brought it, or summoned it to come.

Seconds before, only Kari and the medical staff had been in the room. But the instant she died, this . . . *angel* appeared, as if straight from God. The One the doctor had spent his life denying. The God he refused to believe in. Like a piercing light, the knowledge that the angel had come to protect Kari, that she was to live and do more with her life, stabbed the surgeon's heart. He was only an onlooker to this bigger thing. His duty was to see that she survived.

Leaping to begin resuscitations, the OR team frantically mobilized to bring her back. One minute, two, the efforts went on while the angel stood above them, tall and majestic, waiting.

Three minutes. And life returned. Heart. Pulse. Blood Pressure. And the angel was gone.

As soon as Kari stabilized, the surgical team bent to work. Three doctors were assigned to act as a unit, putting the bone and flesh of her leg back together, while the head surgeon himself began repairing the femoral artery which was ready to tear at any moment, hoping he could save the crucial blood vessel and thus, the avenue of life to her lower limb. With care and precision they slowly reattached her leg until they felt it was complete.

Kari of course knew nothing of this. She awoke dopey and disorientated after coming out of the anesthesia.

"I sort of came to in my room," said Kari. "The first thing I thought of was, did they take my leg off? But I was too groggy to focus enough to look and see.

"The surgeon came into my room and I thought I'd lost my leg because his face was white, and he said, 'I don't want to hear any complaining out of you, Kari. You expired in that room for three minutes, and there was a-a-a-an . . .

a-a-a-an-gel . . . above the bed.' He could barely get the words out. 'You are one lucky girl to be alive,' he said. 'You have a larger purpose in this life than losing your leg.'

"I recall that he told me his wife had terminal cancer, and he didn't believe in God, and seeing an angel above me had challenged all he knew as a doctor.

"So I thought, *they took off my leg.*

"But when I fully came to, I looked down, and I still had it. I remembered what the surgeon had said and I decided, 'Ok, it's about purpose then.'

"After that time, I really started to take life seriously, and I asked God, 'What is my purpose, what is my purpose in life?'

"That's when I decided to stop tinkering with my mouse repellent and turn it into a business and devote my life to service, by helping other people through a purpose-driven business. Now I need more plants than I can grow myself, so instead of growing my own plants, I buy them from other farmers and women who raise them for me.

"After seeing the angel, the surgeon changed his entire life. He moved back to England, where he was raised and had become a doctor. In retrospect, it was very significant for me," she said, "but I think now maybe it was all about saving his life."

So it was that Kari's angel altered the life of not only one, but two persons here on earth. Did God send the angel with a double mandate, to turn the life of both the surgeon and Kari around? Or did he wish to awake the spirit of a man who worked with life and death every day, but who refused to acknowledge the Creator of life, the one who put the breath in our body, the light in our soul? Is it possible that God had a larger purpose for him as well, but that the clay which held his heart tight had to be broken in order for him to see it? I do not know. But I would venture that he held close to him till the end of his days the startling vision of the angel in the operating room. And that he never denied God again.

PATTI

Patti's vibrant energy always surprised me whenever I had to go to the MAF (Medical Assistance Facility) in our home town of Circle, the quick tap-tap of her heels on the vinyl floor as she hurried down the hall, white lab coat swinging over a cheery blouse, stethoscope perpetually wrapped around her neck. As the physician's assistant for our community, she wore the cloak of both doctor and care-taker, often arriving at the nursing home early in the morning to check elderly patients, before putting in a full day at the MAF seeing others.

Though the mother of grown children, Patti was still slender as a teenager, with smooth ivory skin and long dark hair brushing her shoulders. An air of quiet authority put her patients at ease when she entered their room, her deep brown eyes concentrating with a light of compassion as she listened to each person's woes. From ailing widow ladies to big husky farm boys, everyone was treated the same, her natural kindness nourished from a deep love of God.

As the sole practitioner in town, her phone was also the first to ring whenever an accident occurred. More times than I will ever know, she'd worked desperately through the night to keep accident victims alive, staying at the MAF until they could be stabilized or transported out to a larger hospital, then walking through the doors of the office the next morning as if she'd never been disturbed. I knew this from my own experience of becoming suddenly ill, and have heard it more than once from others in town.

The admonition of Jesus to *love thy neighbor as thy-self* was exemplified in Patti's concern for her patients. I'm quite sure she could have easily been that Samaritan told of by Jesus in the tenth chapter of Luke, who, while riding his donkey over the rugged mountains from Jerusalem to Jericho, saw a battered and bloody body lying by the road.

Alarmed, he stopped and slid off the little jenny. Kneeling by the man's side, he carefully rolled him over to see if he was yet alive. Though breathing, the man lay unconscious and badly beaten. The Samaritan immediately saw that without help, the man would surely die.

Stepping to the side of his burro, he took down the goatskin of wine and jug of olive oil. Pouring the wine upon the deepest wounds, he rinsed them until the dirt and soil washed clean, then, before they bled more, dribbled oil over them and quickly bound them with linen cloths. As he worked, the injured man began to groan, rolling his head back and forth while trying to push the Samaritan away.

"No, no!" cried the Samaritan, gripping the man's wrists to keep them at his side. "I am helping you. Don't worry, I'll get you to a safe place where you can rest."

With a sigh, the wounded man relaxed, letting his head fall back upon the stones.

Ah, thought the Samaritan, *he hears me!*

"Listen," he instructed the hurt man. "I must get you up on my donkey. She will carry you. It will be painful, but it must be done."

Turning from the man, he picked up the lead rope of his donkey and tugged her to the side where the man lay.

"Stand now," he ordered the donkey, dropping the rope to the ground. "I must get our friend on you."

Carefully lifting up the hurting man, he slid him onto the donkey's back and pushed one leg over her side. A cry of pain burst from the man's throat as he slumped down and nearly fell off.

"Easy!" cried the Samaritan, grabbing him. "You must stay on."

Holding on to him with one hand, he snagged the donkey's rope with the other and laid it over her neck.

"Come, Little One," he clucked. "Let us go now."

With a twitch of her long ears, the little jenny took one small step and then another, moving onto the solid roadway and down the hillside to safety.

But the Good Samaritan was not satisfied with simply taking the injured man to a roadside inn. He sat by his bed throughout the night, watching to see that he did not worsen, and then paid for his room the next morning when he prepared to leave, asking the innkeeper to care for him until he returned from his business in Jericho, at which time he would pay for all of the expenses.

Yes, I mused, as I finished reading the story of the Good Samaritan and closed my Bible. That is exactly what Patti would do. Stop by the side of the road and doctor anyone who needed it. It was just the way she was made.

One day Grace, an elderly patient of Patti's, came to see her at the MAF. For years, Patti had taken care of Grace's medical needs, becoming good friends with her in the process.

"Each fall she and her husband would go south for the winter with the snowbirds," she told me. "When they came back to Circle in the spring, she'd come in and we'd kind of tune-up whatever was bothering her."

As Grace grew older, different ailments started to affect her, one year it was her lungs, another her heart, then arthritis set into her joints, making them painful and difficult to physically do things. Whatever it was, Patti would immediately begin to treat her and give her relief. "By the time she was ready to depart in the fall, she would be feeling awesome!" smiled Patti, almost as if she still couldn't quite believe how much better Grace had become.

Patti's sympathetic care of Grace impressed her so much that she held every confidence in her. "She always thought I could fix it," explained Patti, in a sort of wondering tone. "That I could make it better and bring her back to health."

But one winter, while driving down the road in a mountainous region of the state in which they lived, Grace and her husband suffered a serious car accident. Their vehicle ran off the highway and plunged down a steep embankment, toward a river flowing under a tall bridge. The wreck knocked her husband out, leaving him slumped over the wheel, unconscious. They finally came to a stop at the base of the bridge, with Grace shaking all over from fear and shock. As she slowly gathered her wits, she began to look around and realized that their car sat too far under the bridge to be seen by anyone on the road above.

For a moment, she just sat there dazed, scared for her husband who was hurt and needed help, and frightened that no one would find them. *What could she do?* Over seventy years old, she knew it was impossible for her to climb up the steep bank, that she did not have the strength to get to the highway, yet how long would it take for somebody to discover the accident if she didn't try? She had to do something.

Still trembling, she pushed open the door and carefully lifted out one foot. Hanging onto the door of the car, she pulled herself out of the seat and stepped out. Feeling helpless and terribly afraid, she stood quivering by the side of the car, wringing her hands in desperation. *What can I do? What can I do?* Only the murmur of the water answered her as it glided down the river. Craning her neck, she peered up the long slope towards the highway, trying to decide what to do, when suddenly, she saw a figure standing on top of the bridge. And that figure was a woman!

As she watched in amazement, the woman walked down the side of the bank as if it was the easiest thing in the world, and came over to Grace. The instant Grace saw her, all fear and anxiety left her. *They were all right! They would be taken care of!* For Grace knew immediately that this woman was a friend.

"I will get you help," the woman said gently. "Just be calm. I need you to sit here and we're going to make sure you get help," she promised her.

Then the woman walked over to the car to check on her husband, noting that while he was still unconscious, he was breathing naturally and did not look to be in any danger.

Going back to Grace, she reassured her again. "Don't worry," she said, "everything is going to be ok, so just wait here now, Grace. I will go and make sure you get help," she reiterated. "So don't be worried."

Great peace and thankfulness flooded Grace's heart as the woman turned to climb back up the steep side of the road ditch and stopped to wait at the side of the highway. Grace watched her stand there until the next vehicle drove by, a semi-truck which the woman flagged down. Immediately the driver called for assistance and within a short time paramedics and the ambulance arrived.

Quickly they carried their equipment down the slope to assess the condition of Grace and her husband, then took them up to the ambulance, one at a time. Frantically Grace looked around for the woman who had helped them. And even though she asked the EMTs, no one had seen her.

Because Grace had an injury to her knee, both she and her husband were admitted to the hospital, where they were cared for before being discharged to go home. The next spring, when they returned to Circle for the summer, Grace went to the MAF to see Patti. But this time she was not there for treatment. She had gone to give Patti a gift.

Sitting in the chair in her office, Grace told Patti all about the accident, how she had been so frightened and unable to do anything, and the woman who came to help them. Then, handing her a small box, she said, "Here is a gift I bought for you. I want you to open it."

Surprised, Patti slipped her finger under the ribbon, pulled it free and then loosened the wrapping, to find a figurine of an exquisite angel nestled in the box. With tears washing down her face, Grace looked up at Patti and smiled. "You see, Patti," she said, "the angel that helped me . . . was you."

Incredulous, Patti stared at Grace.

"But that's not possible," she stammered, quick tears catching at her throat. "It couldn't have been . . . it *wasn't me* . . . because I've been *here*!" Her thoughts flashed to the extreme distance between Circle and that mountain road, easily a thousand miles away, and the fact that she had not been away from the MAF at that time of year.

"No," said Grace. "You were that woman who helped me. You were my angel."

"It couldn't have been *me*!" argued Patti. "It must have been somebody who *looked* like me."

"That's right, she did," said Grace, as she described her. "She had long dark hair, she talked like you, she consoled me like you have, she gave me the peace of mind I needed, to wait for help. It was you." In every way, the woman could have been Patti's twin.

"It was not a vision," assured Grace. "She was there, and disappeared as soon as she got help. In fact, I kept asking the EMTs, 'Where's Patti? Where's Patti?' And they did not know who I was talking about."

"There's no one here," they told me.

"'Well, she was *here,*' I said. 'She was *here.*' I know they thought I was crazy," she smiled through her tears. "That I had bumped my head or something. But I *saw* that woman flag the truck down. And the trucker said that he *was* flagged down, that there was a lady standing by the road, but they could never find her again."

As mysteriously as she had come, the woman disappeared, leaving no trace of her having been there. No car left empty on the bridge, which might have shown she'd stopped while driving by. No footprints on the grassy slope of the ditch. No explanation of how she had known Grace's name while talking to her. No rationale of how she could have vanished in the midst of EMTs, the truck driver, and Grace who were all looking for her. As Grace explained it to Patti, "She was simply gone."

For the rest of Grace's life, the identity of the woman would remain unsolved, with Patti convinced the woman had been an angel, deliberately formed in Patti's likeness to comfort and assist Grace in her frightening circumstances. An angel sent by God who knew exactly what Grace needed in that time of deep distress.

While Grace remained certain the woman was indeed her beloved doctor somehow miraculously transported from the little town of Circle to that bridge over the water so far away. Like the Good Samaritan of long ago, stopping by the side of the road to help the injured traveler, before going on his way.

And though neither one will ever be able to confirm their belief, the alabaster angel given to Patti by Grace continues to stand on her desk in the MAF, a reminder at every glance of her old friend Grace, and the mysterious wonders and glories of God.

PAM

I pushed open the old-fashioned door of the health food store in Lewistown and stepped inside. The delicate fragrance of herbal teas, rich essential oils, and perfumed soaps and creams swirled around me. Drawing the aroma deep into my lungs, I couldn't help but smile. The place smelled like heaven.

Only one other time had I been in this shop, a year before when Milton and I had driven over to watch our granddaughters play basketball. How surprised and pleased I'd been to discover a nook holding my most favorite tea in the world. *Evening in Missoula.* A unique mixture of dried leaves, flowers, and bark gathered from many different plants, *Evening in Missoula* had been created by a small tea and spice company nestled in the middle of the Rocky Mountains in Missoula, Montana. Unfortunately, their tea was not sold in the eastern part of the state where we lived, so I looked for it whenever we went to a town nearer the Rockies. Like Lewistown. Today we were back for a volleyball game, and this time our daughter, Jeannie had come along too, so she could see her girls play.

Creativity abounded in the little store. Jeannie followed

close behind me as we drifted towards the back, stopping frequently to look closer at the many handmade items. Bright cotton aprons hanging from pegs in the kitchen department, thick hand knitted woolen socks stacked on a wooden chair, beautifully pieced quilts, draped over the corner of a an old pine table. Pausing by a rack displaying delicate notecards, I glanced up to meet the smiling blue eyes of a petite blonde-haired lady.

"Can I help you?" she said.

Her inquiry jolted me back to why we were in Lewistown, and the fact that the volleyball game was scheduled to begin shortly. We had to get going.

"Do you have any *Evening in Missoula* tea?" I asked quickly.

"Oh," her face lit up. "Yes, we do. It is so good, isn't it?"

Swiftly, she led me over to a tall narrow bookcase whose shelves were filled with the slender paper sacks of the Montana Tea and Spice Company. I reached for two with the bright green labels displaying *Evening in Missoula* and started toward the counter.

I should ask her about angels.

A niggle of surprise jumped inside me. Just that morning, when we'd decided to go to Lewistown, I'd asked God if He would give me an angel story while we were there. And immediately felt foolish. We were two hundred miles away. Who did I know in Lewistown? No one. How could I ask a stranger? *Where* would I? Was I to approach the parents in the gymnasium, bother the teenager selling hamburgers at McDonald's? And have them wonder if I was insane?

I glanced out the big glass window where Milton waited in the car, then back to Jeannie standing beside me. We really didn't have time. The game was going to start in minutes and I'd stopped only because the store would be closed when we got out.

You must ask her if she's ever seen an angel. Very gently, the words sounded in my mind and pulled my dithering to a halt. I knew that voice. Recognized the steel in it even if it was clothed in velvet.

My soul drew down and stilled as I turned to study the lady behind the till. Middle aged. Happy, open face. Cordial. Friendly. A ranch woman I'd bet, as I watched her capable hands. Strong. Sure. Hands used to working. They'd probably pulled barbed wire and opened many a gate. Held on to life and quite possibly death. The joy of raising animals on a ranch, favorite horses, dogs, even cows, often ended in heartbreaking loss.

Her eyes lifted to mine again, and I gauged their clear blue depth. Would she take exception to such a question, or just consider me a crackpot? I had no choice. Angels might not be everyday topics in this store, but was it better to ignore God or do His bidding? Well, I sure knew the answer to *that* question.

"Ma'am," I hesitated, still not wanting to ask but knowing I had to. "Um, I wonder, do you know anyone who has ever seen an angel?"

A lightning swift change passed over her face, startling me with its intensity. Her eyes, both incredulous and questioning, bore into mine, judging my honesty, my sincerity. Seeking the reason for asking. This was not an ordinary question after all, and who was I but an unknown stranger standing at her till? Then, as if coming to a decision, her shoulders drooped and she answered.

"Yes," she said quietly. "I saw an angel once."

A breath I didn't know I'd been holding whooshed ever so quietly into the scent laden air.

"Could you . . . um . . . tell me about it?" I ventured.

"It was at church," she explained. "We have a little church in Winifred, and I was sitting there one Sunday, sort of feeling sorry for our church and how small it was, and I looked up and there was an angel filling the sanctuary."

Tears glistened in her eyes, threatening to break and fall on the package of tea still in her hand. "See," she tried to laugh, hands fluttering above the counter, "after all this time, it still makes me cry, he was so big, so magnificent."

The relief of hearing her words, of obeying God and not being chastised for it swept through me. God *did* know what He was doing. He had taken me down the street in Lewistown and answered my prayer in a manner I would have never thought possible. With the first person I spoke to. The blue-eyed lady in the heavenly shop, selling tea.

The little church in Winifred stood on the corner where it had been rolled across town over fifty years before. For two days, the hard working men of the community, many of them husky Norwegians, gathered up shovels and left their farms and ranches to spade out the dirt for the basement and foundations by hand. Because the church was going to be the top half of a building which had been used as a town hall, they then jacked up the two stories of the hall and removed the support posts and lower walls so the top level stood clear.

Laying a short track of railroad ties, they placed lengths of iron pipe, four inches in diameter, on top of the ties and lowered the building to rest upon them. Tying on with a big-wheeled steam engine, normally used to thresh their crops of wheat and oats during harvest, the men slowly pulled the building ahead as the pipes turned underneath it. When each span of ties and pipe rolled clear behind the hall, the men picked them up and hauled them around to the front to lay a new stretch.

For three days they worked, inching the structure through the small town until they reached the newly dug basement and could set it down. Although much work still needed to be done on the building, the pride, joy, and satisfaction of getting their church moved was so keen, the parishioners could not wait to hold services. On March 29, 1931, that was what they did, with over forty people attending.

Pam knew the story well, for it had been her husband's grandmother and mother who pined for a Lutheran church in Winifred and worked diligently to bring it into the area. Since then, the family had worshipped there. But by the early 1980s, they were the only ones of a few who continued to do so. With a dwindling away of the townsfolk of Winifred and the surrounding communities, the little church lost many members and was eventually forced to join with three other denominations to keep one place of worship open.

"The congregation had gotten to the point where there were maybe half a dozen people there on Sunday," said Pam. "And sometimes, that was mostly us! I was in my early thirties at the time, and had come to the Lord and asked Him for his Holy Spirit, so I might be able to read his Word and understand it. I was so excited, but I felt like my little church was less than exciting and thought, *Well, Lord, I certainly need to get out of here and go someplace where I can get more training and teaching.* Our church was *so* tiny, it was very discouraging."

Pam also worried about the effect such a small number of parishioners might have on her children. How could it be good for them, when they made up the whole congregation? They would grow up thinking nobody went to church.

Her distress grew to the point of wondering if she and her husband should take their children to a larger parish where they could attend classes with other children. Until God impressed upon her otherwise.

You will come and sit in this pew as long as your husband will come and sit in this pew. You will not *go anywhere else. As long as your husband is willing to come here and worship and take communion, you will not leave.*

Words Pam could not ignore.

In the midst of this spiritual turmoil, Pam read a scripture in Revelation which told about angels of the churches. Now, she was familiar with references to guardian angels, she knew that God will send angels to guard over people. But churches? Never before had such an idea entered her head. How could it be? Was it possible that a church as small as theirs could have an angel dedicated to watching over it?

"I was kind of crying before the Lord in church one Sunday," she remembered, "thinking, *Oh no! Surely there's not an angel here! For six people in the church!* I felt so broken hearted and shamed for this sweet little church my husband's grandmother and mother had built up, that I was almost in tears, and I asked Him, 'Is there really? Surely there's not really an angel for *this* church?'

"And I'm telling you," she said, her voice catching as if it was still too great a thing of which to speak, "I just glanced up, and I *saw,* this enormous, winged being. Wing tip to wing tip, side to side, he filled the whole roof part of our little church, up against the ceiling. I remember feeling like I couldn't hardly *look*. It was absolutely breathtaking.

"And huge! I don't know how long that building is, but he was the height and length of the room, just sort of suspended horizontally across the top of the chapel with his feet towards the altar, looking down on us. His wings seemed to expand to take in the whole width of the church. It was like we were sheltered under them," she added softly, with a little laugh of pure joy.

The angel made no sound, no effort to speak or move as Pam sat riveted below. "It was almost supernatural," she explained, "because it was like the ceiling of the church disappeared, and I could only see *him*. I was so floored, I couldn't hardly take it in. There he was. And he was awesome."

"I did not notice any color associated with what he was wearing, but I remember his face, how handsome and masculine looking it was," she went on. "And the feathers. On his wings. Yes, there were *feathers* on his wings! I could see them. Clear and distinct.

"I was so shocked I couldn't believe it. It was the last thing I expected, to be shown this angel, because that's what it felt like to me. That God was showing me He was there. And I realized there really *was*, that God had provided an angel for our church."

From that point on, Pam discarded all her concerns

about the size of the church and instead, started praying for it constantly. *Bring in a Spirit-filled, godly person to the pulpit,* she asked. *Let him show the congregation how to reach out to the children and raise them up to know the Lord.* Day after day, she pleaded even though it still seemed impossible that somehow their church might have more members.

"Many Sundays I spent in the church, just praying," she said. "'Oh, thank you, for sending the angel, Lord, but please make it worth his while.' I felt so bad that this beautiful, huge angel would be made available to guard over this little place, and there was hardly anybody there. It seemed . . . *wrong.*"

As the snow melted on the mountains and the calves frolicked in the grass, she prayed. When the leaves of the aspens turned to gold and another year ended, she kept on. Through many different changes to the church, which included giving up a full-time pastor and selling the parsonage, Pam continued her supplications, until almost two decades had passed. Years which had never dimmed her vision of the angel or the hope that God would fill their church, although sometimes she wondered if it would ever happen.

"Then one year we had to call a new pastor," she said, "and He sent us a woman! I could not believe it, it had never seemed right to me to have a woman in the pulpit . . . and she was *wonderful!*

"She went out and visited everybody. She started a

young marrieds group, with some of them becoming the really evangelistic people in our congregation. They started doing things with the children's ministry and others that were just over the top. She was absolutely the most dynamic pastor we've ever had."

To her astonishment, the coming of that unusual minister became the answer to all of Pam's prayers, as more and more members of the community were drawn to the pastor and began to attend the little church. Today, more than thirty years after seeing the glorious angel and beginning to pray for a greater membership, the church is crammed with families and little ones when Pam goes to worship on Sundays. Children under ten years old easily make up a third of the congregation, and often the folding doors leading to an added-on hall have to be opened for extra seating.

"I can't tell you how thrilling it's been," she grinned. "Our sanctuary probably holds seventy people if it was packed full, which it sometimes is. Not every Sunday, because people will be out moving cows or getting their seeding done. But I feel like our angel has his hands full now.

"It has made me realize that it was worth hanging in there. To pray, and keep on praying. And as God answered those requests, He'd be glorified in that place and people would know Him."

Pam has never seen the angel again, nor has she asked to. "I feel like it's none of my business," she explained. "I've always assumed God would show us what we *needed* to see. But I think," she continued, "if we were made aware of what's really around us all of the time, if we could recognize that we are just a shadow of the real thing, I don't know if we could hardly function at all."

Surrounded by the magnificent angels of God.

MARJORIE

Who in the world could that be? I wondered, hurrying from the living room as the doorbell rang.

A blast furnace of heat hit me when I pushed the screen door open to see an elderly man standing on the step, thin and sweating in the hundred degree sun, his ragged shirt streaked with grease and dirt. I'd never seen him before in my life.

His eyes lifted to mine, and in that instant he stated in pure, honest fact.

"You are a Whitmer. I used to dandle you on my knee."

Astonished, I stared at the stranger. How many years had it been since I'd heard that old-fashioned word—*dandle,* which brought a flash of a laughing baby, bouncing on a knee covered with striped denim overalls. And who was this man that knew my name, one I had not used in thirty years. Ever since the day of my marriage. He obviously knew *me.*

"Please." I said, pulling the door wide. "Come in."

He stepped into the hall and stopped, refusing to go further. I motioned for him to keep on. "No, no," he said, wheezing slightly. "I just need some gas. My pickup ran out of gas on the road."

"But you're hot," I argued. "Can I get you some lemonade? I'm sorry," I apologized, "I don't know your name."

His eyes came back to me and for the first time he seemed to relax. Like an old dog who wobbles to his rug and circles with a sigh, he walked to the table and sank down on a chair, his arms falling at his sides.

"I'm Joe Benes," he said, and all those pages to yesterday flipped back to our house in Circle and Daddy welcoming his friend from Richey. He would have known us, all us kids, and most especially my sister and me, who were the talk of the country when we were born. Mother always said everyone came to marvel. Twins! Joe would have been one, and I'm sure he did dandle us on his knee.

The responsibility to honor this man strengthened my resolve.

"What can I get you?" I insisted, bound to give him the hospitality I knew Mother would have, any time he came to see us.

"Just water," he replied. "Could I have a glass of cold water?"

The simplest request on earth. To anyone who has been thirsty, nay, more so, parched beyond thought, weaving under the baking heat of a burning sun, the most common element on earth becomes more valuable than sacks of gold. It is life. Nothing stands in its place.

I reached for the ice cubes and dropped them in a tall glass. Then I filled it with chilled water and set it on the table before him. He stretched out a hand and curled his fingers around it, soaking in the cool damp before lifting it to his mouth to drink. I watched him savor each swallow, saw the deep breath he took in relief as he put the glass down and leaned back against the chair.

Then ever so softly he said, "Thank you."

Like so many things, that last time I got to see Joe Benes faded and disappeared until some years later, when a chance meeting with my friend, Marjorie, reminded me of the priceless value of water, as I walked down the aisles of our little grocery store, perfectly happy, singing along with Marty Robbins on the sound system. "El Paso." Who could resist that tragedy of love and loss?

Just as I took down a new box of teabags, I glanced up and saw Marjorie turning the corner at the end of the row. One of those people who is filled with kindness, she had an ability to make everyone around her feel better. Including myself. Smiling, she stopped her cart in the aisle and asked.

"Are you still writing angel stories?"

Her question caught me off guard, until I remembered calling her to verify Grandma Massar's story about Alice's angels.

"Yes," I said, grinning too. "I sure am."

"You know, Wanda," she said, the barest hint of excitement and awe edging her voice, "I saw an angel once. It was hot, hot! August, I think. He came to my house and I gave him a glass of cold water."

A little ding sounded in my brain, like that doorbell heralding the visit of Joe Benes so long before. *An angel.* I thought. *Cold water.* This I would have to hear. Because as sure as the sun rises, and sets in the west, I knew God had handed me another angel story. Unexpected, unbidden, unasked. Not chance at all.

Like most of the kids around our town, Marjorie had been raised on the farm. With living 18 miles from town, it was difficult for the family of ten to get in for Sunday Services. When their country school closed, they moved into town for the school year. Marjorie was ten years old by then and Sunday School at the Lutheran Church became an important part of her life. When she became old enough, she sang in the choir and joined Luther League.

While her father tilled the weeds out of his soil and prayed for rain to grow his crops, those years of Marjorie's youth watered her faith and grew deep, strong roots that would uphold her for the rest of her life. To the time when she lost her first husband in a tragic accident. And then her second as well.

But Marjorie was not prone to depression. Gray clouds could hardly compete against her natural sunny disposition. Still, the loss was great and occasionally it affected her spirits, sometimes without her even realizing it. By the time of her angel story, Marjorie had moved to a house in town which had a porch, fortunate because as is so common in Montana, August turned off blistering hot. That day she'd just put two chairs outside to make a comfortable place to sit out of the heat, when an old man stopped at her door.

"He had snow white hair and was walking with a limp," she recalled. "He carried a cane and told me his hips were bad."

Marjorie wondered why he would be out on such a hot day, and he explained that his son was going to be running for an office and he was passing out brochures for him. Marjorie never saw the brochures.

The old fellow was hot and tired. Seeing the chairs on her porch, he looked at her and asked, "May I sit down for a moment?"

"Of course," Marjorie told him, gesturing to one of the chairs. "You sit right here. May I get you a glass of cold water?" she added.

The stranger responded with obvious relief.

"Oh," he said, "that would be so wonderful."

Marjorie went right to the kitchen and got the water for him and then sat down to visit.

"It must have been ten minutes or so, just talking about normal things," she said, "and I was listening to him . . . looking at him, and Wanda," she said, her voice slowing down to enunciate each separate word, "he had the deepest, deepest blue eyes that I've ever seen in anyone."

Just the memory of them caused Marjorie to catch her

breath. "It was almost as if you could see to the bottom of a crystal clear, beautiful pool. The very bottom," she said. "And his hair was *white*. It was not the graying type, but a full head of nice hair as white as snow."

In addition to those striking features, Marjorie noticed his smooth, unlined face, so unusual in older people. "You know how your skin gets by the time you reach that age," she noted, "but his skin was *beautiful*, not wrinkled at all. And it was nicely tanned."

Many of us have been around enough older folks to know that loss of skin color also accompanies old age. Often it becomes sallow, faded out to a pasty white. Sometimes freckles and age spots begin to cover it. Others show a high degree of yellow pigmentation which makes you wonder if the person is suffering from jaundice.

The stranger had none of these. In fact, Marjorie remarked again, "He had such a *kind, gentle* face. This is what so impressed me," she explained. "Those kind eyes and a sort of soft, gentle voice. To me a very caring voice," she elaborated.

"He was wearing a blue shirt," she went on, "and was dressed in regular cool summer clothing, it wasn't anything out of the ordinary, and he was not real tall. Not a big man," she said. As many men in our community are.

For a little while longer, Marjorie continued to talk with the stranger until he said, "Well, it's time I need to be going on."

"I just said goodbye, stepped in the house and looked out my window," she explained, "and he was *gone*. I looked in either direction, around the trees that line my walkway because he was walking slow, and he was nowhere in sight. It's quite a ways down to the street from my house, and he just *disappeared.*

"It was impossible," she said, with a catch in her throat. "And it hit me, right in my heart that he was an angel. It thrilled me to its depths."

Of its own accord, her hand lifted and pressed upon her chest. "I don't know if I was having a hard time after I lost my husband or what, but the Lord must have known I needed someone at my door right at that time. And the thought came to me, when I asked if I could give him a glass of cold water, that is in Scripture. *'If you do it for anyone, you do it for me,'* the Lord says. Ah, those precious words of Jesus.

> *Verily I say unto you, Inasmuch as ye have done it unto one of the least of these my brethren, ye have done it unto me.* Matthew 25:40

The joy in Marjorie bubbled out in a happy laugh, and I was reminded of the apostles at Pentecost filled with the Holy Ghost, dancing and singing in delirious joy, speaking in other tongues, languages they did not know, filled with so much happiness that the men who rushed to see this wonder, accused them of being drunk on new wine. They were not, but rather with the same Spirit of the Lord, joy poured out upon Marjorie.

"It just thrilled me for so long afterwards," she continued, "and even when I think of it today visiting with you, I can still feel in my heart that he was an angel for me. It has made me so thankful and given such peace." She could not keep the tears from her eyes.

"It also gave me a broader depth of what the Lord is, how the Lord works, and how much He does love us. Many have seen angels, have had the angels come, but oh, the protection we have, we don't realize how we've been protected, how we are *being* protected. No one can tell me there are not angels around us at all times. There are. It is wonderful."

Amen

EPILOGUE

Who could have known that across the hills of Montana there would be so many angels? Appearing to my family. Friends. Old neighbors and new. Strangers I had yet to meet. Or that others who had left our state would have the angels follow along, to succor, uphold and lend comfort, when all seemed lost and hopeless. How can I thank those ones who were so kind as to share their stories with me for this book? It feels impossible, but I do from the bottom of my heart and pray God to bless them always.

For a long time, I didn't think I needed to ask people if they had seen an angel, because I thought God would present them to me, rather like He did with the surprise of Rhonda, totally out of the blue. But work on the book, and being prompted to inquire when I least expected it, caused me to change my mind and realize I too had a job to do in order to fulfill His assignment, and it started with asking, many times of strangers. Even if it made me appear to be dumb or stupid or foolish or insane.

How many times have we heard the phrase, *He is a fool for God*? Meaning, a person who will do anything when seeking to obey the Lord, no matter what humanity thinks about it or how they might judge him. And slowly I realized that description applied to me. So I came to learn that it was all right when someone looked at me, wondering, and I knew what that wondering was. I strove to be gracious when questioned and answer truthfully. And became joyful when a light of kinship lit someone's eyes and they nodded, without saying a word.

Some stories distressed me. Like the old man, wizened and thin, with a grizzled beard reaching down his neck, looking as if he could step into the boots of a Civil War General, so spare and somehow courtly he was, standing on the lawn of the city's park, telling me he was from New Jersey, living now with his daughter and grandchildren in Montana, and that when a young boy, he had seen an angel.

A remembrance which caused him to look off into the spreading branches of the cottonwood above us and slightly shake his head, murmuring, "He just flew off, without a sound." Before coming back to earth and saying so seriously, "I have never told anyone about it." And I, with a pang in my heart, was unable to keep from asking, "Not even your parents?"

Immediately, the old man stiffened and drew himself up, falling back a half step as if he had been struck. "My parents!" he exclaimed, with both a scoff and disbelief. "They would never have believed me!" And my soul lurched for that little boy, just sitting in the quiet night, full of peace before going to bed, unable to share this unexpected gift from God with the most important people in his life. His mother and father. Having to hold it in until his old age when he felt safe—safe enough to confide in a stranger who had shown she would believe him.

Indignation flamed within me for those two parents, commissioned with the duty to respect and nurture their child but who refused to do so. What difference did it make how *they* thought? Fact is fact, and the sight of what their son instantly recognized as an angel of God was as real to him as their own bodies. That he knew he could not trust them, had to instead protect himself from them, showed how miserably he was treated.

Just then, shouts of "Grandpa!" fell on our ears as two little girls came rushing over the grass toward us. Silently the old man turned and walked away, disappearing into the crowd with them dancing on each side, clutching his hands as if they could not let him go, while I stayed behind, praying that before he left this earth, he would tell them, too, of that long ago day when he sat on the steps and watched an angel fly up into the star-filled sky. With silver moonbeams shining on his wings.

Or the pastor, beyond middle age like I am, handing out reprints of the Book of John to anyone who walked by at the Christmas bazaar. Tired, defeated, somewhat befuddled, he slumped in the metal folding chair and listlessly watched the bustling shoppers. I wished I could help him. Lift him up somehow. After all, Christmas is the most joyous time of the year, more important even, to me, than Easter, for without the birth of the Christ child, there would have been no Easter morning. And it was the angels who announced his coming to the shepherds. To us. The common folk of the world. Not the kings and rulers.

Perhaps he knows of an angel.

I stopped and took the little, blue book he held up. Turning the pages I thanked him and quietly asked, "Would you by any chance know someone who has seen an angel?" His eyes stilled, then he actually looked at me and soberly shook his head, almost as if he was apologizing for something he should be able to do. He is a minister no less, who cannot feed his flock, this one of God's people who asks for such a little thing. Confirmation of His majesty and glory.

"No, no," he spoke softly, unwilling to admit to his failure. "My brother saw our brother once, who had passed on before, but an angel, no I have never seen an angel or know one who has." And to my astonishment and grief, he turned away from me, dismissing my presence in as certain a manner as if he had given a shouted command. "Be gone!" And I slunk away, having failed in my mission as well.

But the pastor's mention of his brothers reminded me of questions several people had asked concerning the difference between seeing angels and a person who had died. Some wondered if they were the same, others feared they were hallucinating or verging on insanity. After all, it is not really normal to look up and see the form of a person you know has passed away. Could one somehow return and be seen again here on earth?

Actually, yes. The startling experience of my cousin Gail showed how quickly and easily it can happen, when our Uncle Mac strode past her after his death. I thought it interesting that though only a child, she knew he had died, and acknowledged it those many years later. It showed me how closely our spirit is tied to the things of God's world, but it sees with eyes mostly hooded, often sheltering us from mysteries too deep and powerful for our minds to absorb. It does not mean however, that the mysteries do not happen.

I walked into the room at the nursing home where my mother lay on the bed, shortly after her brother, Spike, had passed away. He was an old cowboy, who worked as a ranch hand when he came back from serving in the Navy during WWII. Both Mom and Spike had been raised on the ranch in Montana where my grandfather ran Hereford cattle. Although she was two years younger, Mom had graduated from high school the same year he did.

Spike was very introspective and did not talk much. The night sky was his passion and over the course of his lifetime he wrote three books about the stars. Mother always worried about Spike because he never married and had no one to care for him. Losing him was going to be hard as he was the last of her family. It was the reason why I'd gone over, to make sure she was all right.

Mom glanced up when I came through the door, a

smile of greeting lighting her face as I bent down to give her a hug. For a little while we talked about the kids and what everyone was doing, then she settled back against the pillows and caught my eye in that peculiar way she had when trying to decide if she should tell me something a little strange. I waited, giving her time to make up her own mind without pressure from me. Never dreaming of what she would say.

"Spike came to see me one night."

Her calm, level voice shocked me as much as the words. This was Mother, who sat with us in the chapel for Spike's funeral. She knew he was dead, but acted like he'd just dropped in for coffee.

"Really, Mother!" I blurted out, unable to keep my agitation from showing. Was this a nightmare she'd been having or a dream or a ghost showing up? I had no idea, but the only way to find out was to ask. "What happened, Mom?" I said, forcing myself to quiet down so I could listen carefully to what she had to say.

"Well, I was laying here sleeping," she said. "It was the middle of the night. I woke up and turned my head and looked, and there was Spike, standing by my bed." She paused a moment and raised her arm to point about three quarters of the way down the side. "Right there."

"What did he look like?" I asked, when she stopped speaking.

"O-o-oh." Involuntarily her eyelids closed and a kind of gentle sigh went through her whole body as she said with a combination of amazement and pride. "He was wearing brand new Levi's and a brand new Levi jacket."

All those terrible years of the 1930s rushed to me. When ranchers burned off the spines on cactus to keep their cattle from starving. When dust storms blew up on the wind, obliterating the sun. When no grass grew, and no rain fell, and hope died with every dry, blistering day. The years Mom and Spike had lived through on the ranch, doing without. Such extravagance as new Levi's could only be yearned for.

But even if they were mended and patched, handed down from neighbors or friends, Spike wore the garb of cowboys. Jeans from blue denim. Long-sleeved, cotton shirts with pockets to hold Bull Durham sacks of tobacco. Boots with high heels to fit a stirrup. He never relinquished them. Until his death, he dressed in western shirts with yokes and snaps, Levi jeans, and lace-up leather boots. Well-worn and faded, but still serviceable. A quick picture of him standing tall and slim in the stiff jacket and jeans, raven hair combed to one side, craggy face unlined and covered with a big smile, flashed in my mind when Mom said that.

How like God, I thought, *to give him those clothes when he got to heaven.*

"He was young," Mom added, "and he looked wonderful, I could see that he was happy," she said. "He wanted to tell me he was all right. I reached out my hand to him," she motioned to the side, "but before I touched his arm, he said, 'No,' and then he was gone."

From that time, Mother never worried about Spike. His visit brought her great comfort. No longer was she concerned about his well-being, because she knew he was happy and contented where he was, and her days of caring for him were over. How could I doubt her telling?

This revelation from Mother corroborated an experience of one of my friends who not only once, but twice, saw her father after his death. Sharon was only four years old when her father was unexpectedly killed in a car accident. The loss threw both her mother and Sharon into turmoil.

"We were living in Alabama, and my mother made a quick decision to move back to Indiana and buy a house right across the street from one of her best friends. My poor mother," she said, with heartbreak in her voice, "she couldn't decide what she wanted to do with her life after this terrible, terrible thing happened. And I was absolutely petrified to let her out of my sight."

Sharon's mother seemed to instinctively know how desperately her children needed her, and seldom left them, but for some reason, she had to be away one evening and called a babysitter to watch over them while she was gone.

"My sisters and I were upstairs and I had gone to bed," said Sharon. "I was supposed to be asleep, so I can remember lying in bed and all of a sudden, my father was just *there*, at my side. It was like he just appeared.

"My father was very handsome, he had beautiful blue eyes and wavy, thick hair and a high forehead. His grandparents were German so he was very German looking. He did not even begin to learn English until he went to school. I immediately recognized him and cried, 'Oh! You're Daddy! Oh! Yeah!'

"I sat up in bed and reached for his hand and he sort of sat down on the bed. My father was a business man, and he was dressed in a business suit and had a briefcase with him like he was going to work. It didn't seem strange to me at all that he should be there. It felt very natural and I was happy to see him.

"He told me, 'Everything is going to be all right. You'll be ok. Your mother is going to be all right.' I wanted to ask him more questions but he said, 'I've really got to go now.'

"It didn't seem odd or out of place or scary, but I felt sad that he was leaving. He was there for such a brief time, just long enough to comfort me and let me know everything was going to be ok.

"When he had gone, I called out for someone and the babysitter came into the room. She must have said something to my mother as soon as she got home, because she came immediately into the bedroom and I told her about it. Mother never dismissed it. She knew I felt it was very real and she did not question it in any way, but I'm sure that in retrospect, it must have been pretty overwhelming to her."

Sharon's father passed away in June of 1955. That first

time he came back to see her occurred during the following winter of 1956. Shortly afterward, her mother decided to move back to Alabama from Indiana, where once again, her father visited Sharon during the summer of 1956.

"It was hot weather and I was in the living room of the home we had moved into," she recalled, "looking at a picture of my mother and father, taken right around the time that they were married. It is a beautiful picture of them, and I have it to this day.

"And as natural as can be, there was my father, standing behind me with his hands on my shoulders. It was a warm summer day and this time he was dressed in a casual shirt and pants. I said, 'Oh, Daddy! Isn't Mommy beautiful?' Because I was looking at that picture.

"And he said, 'Yes, she is. She's just beautiful.'

"'We gotta go tell her!' I said, and went running in the other room to the kitchen where my mother was.

"'Daddy and I want to tell you something!' I exclaimed. I have a vague memory of her being kind of shocked, and then I looked behind me and my father wasn't there. It was just a brief moment in time, and it's never ever happened again."

Regret and sorrow thickened her voice. "I've shared this with people who have tried to explain it away scientifically," she said. "Saying things like . . . 'you wanted him so bad that your mind made this happen.' But it's like 'Noooo.' These experiences are *so real* to me that nobody has ever been able to convince me they didn't really happen. I've always stood grounded on that. But I feel it's something I won't really know the answers to until I cross over myself.

"My sisters were seven and eight, and they did not see him. It's caused me to wonder if perhaps he realized I would have the hardest time with losing him, and he wanted to have a few moments with me to try and help me understand the transition. Seeing him has made me more open to the . . . heavenly world. Knowing it's there and that sometimes we see messages in different things. If someone has an experience of that nature, I don't discount it or try to intellectualize it. I just know that those kinds of things can happen."

Quite clearly, Mother's and Sharon's experiences illustrate the differences between human beings who returned after death to visit their loved ones, and the unexpected and often mysterious appearance of angels. We humans often come as ourselves, as Mother saw with her brother, Spike, and Sharon with her father.

As Sharon explained so eloquently, she intuitively knew the visits from her father were not conjured up from desire or loneliness, nor was he an hallucination. Although she was only four years old, her spirit, her subconscious mind, recognized him as being who he was. Her beloved father. Speaking, walking, talking, just as Jesus did when he appeared before the disciples after his death.

And as they thus spake, Jesus himself stood in the mist of them, and saith unto them, Peace be unto you. But they were terrified and affrighted, and supposed that they had seen a spirit.

And he said unto them, Why are ye troubled? and why do thoughts arise in your hearts? Behold my hands and my feet, that it is I myself: handle me, and see; for a spirit hath not flesh and bones, as ye see me have. Luke 24:36–39

The angels who come to earth with wings are easily recognized. Those without them seem to be a normal human being, usually a stranger, unknown to the party they come to assist. Almost always they are not correctly identified until after their disappearance.

Even in the instance of Grace, who was helped by a woman who looked exactly like her doctor, Patti, back home, it was obvious to Patti that the person had to have actually been an angel, for on the day of the accident, she was in Montana over 1500 miles away and nowhere near the bridge where Grace and her husband ran off the road.

But our God is a Great and Good God, and in 2 Corinthians He warns us that angels can at times, be other than what they seem. There Paul writes that he fears the Christians may be corrupted by the wiles of the serpent, this being Satan, and that they are to be wary of false apostles and deceitful workers, transforming themselves into the apostles of Christ. Why did he caution us so?

> *For Satan himself is transformed into an angel of light.*
> 2 Corinthians 11:14

This tells us that the devil can disguise himself as a fake angel, in order to confuse our minds, and turn our hearts from God. This old firebrand will use any lie to deceive us, but we have an ironclad protection against his imposters, for there is a simple test to determine if the angel is from God or not. John gives us instructions,

> *Beloved, believe not every spirit, but try the spirits whether they are of God: because many false prophets are gone out into the world.*
> *Hereby know ye the Spirit of God: Every spirit that confesseth that Jesus Christ is come in the flesh is of God.* 1 John 4:1–2

So . . . pretty easy. All we have to do is ask the angel, "Did Jesus Christ come in the flesh?"

If he stutters and stammers, changes the subject, or withers upon the spot, cry out to that evil one, "Get thee hence, Satan! In the name of Jesus Christ, be thou cast into the sea!" And he shall be gone. (Mark 11:23)

But if the angel responds that Jesus came in the flesh, you know he has arrived straight from heaven at the behest of God. It is important that we have this information so we can be forearmed and thus defeat the arrows of the enemy. Angels belong to the spiritual realm, and we must acknowledge that. While through our modern age, man has been deluded into thinking that he is a physical creature only, in truth, it is the spirit given him by the Almighty which fills him with life. And it is that spirit which interacts with God's holy messengers, His angels, and which we must use to verify their authenticity for our own safety.

In many ways, I feel like the people who told me their stories invited me into a secret room, one both precious and sacred, held fast by a golden key only they could turn. With the exception of Grandma Strutz, each one willingly shared their experience, many with tears and obvious awe. And no matter the years that had passed or the age of the viewer, to them, it seemed as if it had been only yesterday.

The angels came unbidden, silent. Who could have expected them? And how was it that so many members of my own family had seen angels, and I did not know? My mother. My sister. My cousin. Did they purposefully keep these visions hidden? Were they afraid to tell others? Did they want to try and sort them out, come to some logical conclusion, an explanation they could give and believe at the same time? Did they not wish to be called crazy, or did they simply *know*, within their own soul, which is timeless and full of mystery, as are the angels, that there was no explanation. That whatever they tried to conceive or make up, it would not be truth. For facts speak. And nothing could be added to them to make it more palatable. The angels came. And were.

More Christmases have passed than I want to remember since that morning God sat me down and gave me a job to do. Now it is done. The frigid day Jeannie's baby was born is long past, and he is grown. Healthy, industrious, beginning what I hope to be a life of great happiness. Do angels stand around him? I cannot see, my eyes as they are, covered with clay. But in my heart I'm sure. For God takes care of us. The small, the weak, the infirm. The young, the strong, the brave, the aged. And He always will.

He that dwelleth in the secret place of the most High shall abide under the shadow of the Almighty. I will say of the Lord, He is my refuge and my fortress: my God; in him will I trust. . . . He shall cover thee with his feathers, and under his wings shalt thou trust: his truth shall be thy shield and buckler. . . . For he shall give his angels charge over thee, to keep thee in all thy ways. They shall bear thee up in their hands, lest thou dash thy foot against a stone. Psalm 91:1–2, 4, 11–12

His promise echoes down through the ages. A message of such forgiveness, we can hardly bear.

For God so loved the world, that he gave his only begotten Son, that whosoever believeth in him should not perish, but have everlasting life. John 3:16

The reason for Christmas: Jesus. Come to take our sins. And if we accept him as such, believe in our heart that he is the Son of God, God will shelter us under His wings. For with those words, we dwell in the secret place of the most High.

While His angels stand guard.

QUESTIONS FOR
BOOK CLUBS

1. Have you, like the author, ever been given a job you did not think you could accomplish? Why were you afraid of failing? Did you go ahead and try to do it and succeed, or were you unsuccessful as you had feared?

2. Stories of angels can come from unexpected places, which the author learned from her cousin, Gail. Has anyone ever told you of a time when they saw an angel? Were you surprised? Did you believe them? Why do you think Gail told the author her story?

3. Little girl Alice tells her mother the angels have come to take her home, when she was dying of what the doctor believed was tuberculosis. Reports of people seeing angels when they are near death has become more common in our present day. Why did this experience change Grandma Massar's feelings from sorrow to comfort? Do you think it would help your grief if one you loved saw an angel before they passed away?

4. Miracle workers. Healers. Helpers. Protectors. All of these descriptions have been applied to angels. But no one dreamed Grandma Strutz could be brought back from death's door. Why would an angel come to restore an old woman? One who was content with the many years she had lived, and ready to go back to heaven. How would a miraculous healing such as this affect you, if it happened to someone you knew and loved? Would it bring you closer to God or cause you to ponder the mysteries of heaven?

5. Who can count a mother's love? The times she will send a prayer, to cover her children, to keep them safe. Such as Mary Anne did through the hours of rushing to her son's side after his accident while skiing. Why did God send so many angels to his aid? *Legions* of them. And what caused Him to pull back the veil and allow her to see them, while assuring her that John would be all right. Because He had "other plans" for him. But why did Mary Anne find it so hard to believe Him? Do you think God has special plans for each of us as well?

6. The angel who came to console Michael after his grandmother's death, appeared to be a regular human being, yet he knew things it was impossible for anyone but Michael himself to know, halfway around the world from his home in America. Have you ever heard of an

angel who seemed to be a normal person? Why do you think God sometimes sends them to us in this way, as He states in Hebrews 13:2: *Be not forgetful to entertain strangers: for thereby some have entertained angels unawares.*

7. Most often, we think of angels as tall, white-robed figures with beautiful white wings. Seldom do we consider them as soldiers in God's army, such as Gloria saw when she asked protection for her daughter. How many kinds of angels do you suppose reside in heaven? Why do you think God would send a special type to help us here on earth?

8. Freedom of will. Every person on earth arrives with that gift from God. With it we can choose how to live . . . and what to believe. Or not believe, as Kari's doctor had done all of his life. But when confronted with the glorious, majestic angel above her body, all of his beliefs burst around his feet like dried clay. Have you ever tried to convince an atheist of God? Have you ever wondered yourself if God exists? What do you think this doctor felt when he saw the angel? How would you have?

9. Usually we think of angels as being assigned to a particular person, one on one. But after seeing her sanctuary filled with the huge angel of God, Pam was convinced

God also sends angels for whole buildings, such as the church. Have you ever wondered if your church has its own special angel? How would it change your feelings if you imagined the congregation worshipping under his wings?

10. Can you share with the group if you have ever seen an angel or know someone who has? Or if you've always wanted to see an angel and never have? Have you ever asked God to send an angel to help you or a loved one, and had Him do so, whether you were able to see the angel or not? What is your favorite story of an angel from the Bible and why?

INVITATION

Have you ever seen an angel or know someone who has? If so, I would love to hear about it. Please email me at:

wjross@midrivers.com

ABOUT THE AUTHOR

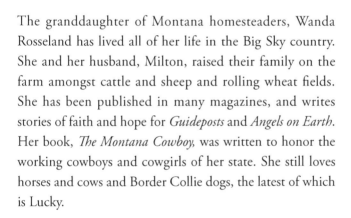

The granddaughter of Montana homesteaders, Wanda Rosseland has lived all of her life in the Big Sky country. She and her husband, Milton, raised their family on the farm amongst cattle and sheep and rolling wheat fields. She has been published in many magazines, and writes stories of faith and hope for *Guideposts* and *Angels on Earth*. Her book, *The Montana Cowboy*, was written to honor the working cowboys and cowgirls of her state. She still loves horses and cows and Border Collie dogs, the latest of which is Lucky.

IF YOU ENJOYED THIS BOOK, WILL YOU CONSIDER SHARING THE MESSAGE WITH OTHERS?

Mention the book in a blog post or through Facebook, Twitter, Pinterest, or upload a picture through Instagram.

Recommend this book to those in your small group, book club, workplace, and classes.

Head over to facebook.com/worthypublishing, "LIKE" the page, and post a comment as to what you enjoyed the most.

Tweet "I recommend reading #AngelsAmongUs by Wanda Rosseland // @worthypub"

Pick up a copy for someone you know who would be challenged and encouraged by this message.

Write a book review online.

WORTHY®
PUBLISHING

Visit us at worthypublishing.com

twitter.com/worthypub

worthypub.tumblr.com

facebook.com/worthypublishing

pinterest.com/worthypub

instagram.com/worthypub

youtube.com/worthypublishing

Made in the USA
Coppell, TX
04 December 2024

41357090R00127